Centre For Business, Arts and Technology
Learning Centre

Centre for Business, Arts
&Technology
444 Camden Road
London N7 0SP
020 7700 8642
LibraryCBAT@candi.ac.uk

CITY AND ISLINGTON
COLLEGE

This book is due for return on or before the date stamped below. You may renew
by telephone. Please quote the barcode number or your student number.
This item may not be renewed if required by another user.

Fine : 10p per day

1 WEEK LOAN

HO   YOU   COD   TE

LAURENCE KING

Published in 2012 by
Laurence King Publishing Ltd
361–373 City Road, London,
EC1V 1LR, United Kingdom
T +44 20 7841 6900
F +44 20 7841 6910
enquiries@laurenceking.com
www.laurenceking.com

Text © 2012 Mark Atkinson

This book was designed and produced by
Laurence King Publishing Ltd, London.

A catalogue record for this book is available
from the British Library

ISBN: 978 1 85669 842 9

Design by Melanie Mues,
Mues Design, London

Front cover: Untitled final collection by
Tsolo Munkh

Back cover: Concept board of Meccano
by Cathy Amouroux

Printed in China

HOW TO CREATE YOUR FINAL COLLECTION

A FASHION STUDENT'S HANDBOOK

MARK ATKINSON

LAURENCE KING PUBLISHING

CONTENTS

Related study material is available
on the Laurence King website at
www.laurenceking.com

INTRODUCTION

The purpose of this book is to assist fashion design students to produce a womenswear capsule collection. This exercise usually takes place during the final year of a fashion design course and is referred to as the degree or final collection. This book provides a step-by-step approach to designing such a collection and is intended to accompany students throughout the process.

Students may also consult this book in the years prior to graduation in order to gain a better understanding of the key skills they will need to acquire to complete their course successfully. This will help put into context the projects and exercises they will have to complete before their final collection.

Finally, this book should prove helpful to anyone interested in the design of a fashion collection, as the processes followed by students and professional designers are very similar. The book is in fact illustrated throughout by work from both student designers and professional designers.

HOW TO USE THIS BOOK

Designing a successful fashion collection requires many different skills. These can be broadly categorized as creative, technical and commercial. Each is developed and cultivated in a different way: a commercial approach requires knowledge of the markets, technical skills improve with practice, and creativity relies on inspiration. The emphasis of this book, however, is the *process* of designing a collection rather than an attempt to address each set of skills in detail.

One of the skills that sets good designers apart is the ability to reflect upon and assess their own creation. Good knowledge of the industry will help you, as you work through every step of the design process, to evaluate your work in this wider context and be prepared to judge when it is not satisfactory.

The notion that the design of a collection, a creative process, can be formalized may be surprising. There is certainly no magic formula. It is possible, however, to break down this process into coherent stages. Your own path may turn out to be slightly different from the ideal route described in this book, and the terms used may vary, but the issues raised and the structure suggested should help you to get a sense of the design process and guide you as it unfolds. This book provides signposts to a journey that is very much a personal one.

Case studies of final collections designed by fashion students from around the world are included at the end of the book and on the accompanying CD-Rom. These case studies illustrate the different stages of the process described in the book, showing a diversity of individual approaches to fashion design, and images of the case study collections are also featured in the chapters.

Each chapter in *How to Create Your Final Collection* explores one step of the design process. Chapters 1 and 2 highlight the context in which designers work – a necessary consideration to deliver a collection that is viable and timely in its design. They highlight different questions that should be considered before refining the collection brief given to you – namely, understanding the market, choosing a season and analysing fashion trends.

Chapter 3, Creative Research, describes the explorative stage, where you research and select one or two themes that will inspire and influence your collection. Evocative material collated on a **theme board** will help you keep in mind those chosen influences during the next stages.

In Chapter 4, Development and Sampling, you will encounter the experimental, playful stage where you generate and test ideas for different aspects of garment design, such as colour range, material, print, surface embellishment, silhouette, **style line** or construction. This work may also help you to formulate the idea of your collection as a *concept*, usually in the form of a **concept** board with text added that explains what your collection is trying to achieve, and a **mood board** that shows how you intend to do so. The concept acts as a guide and maintains the coherence of a collection.

Chapter 5 brings together the different ideas and elements of design retained after development and sampling to produce garment designs. Range planning organizes these garments into a coherent collection and optimizes each completed outfit. Chapter 6 looks at the all-important presentation and styling of your collection for both your submission to the jury and for the catwalk.

Finally, Chapter 7 explains how to include your final collection in your portfolio and suggests ways in which you can extend its use through the development of diffusion lines, enabling you to target your portfolio successfully to potential employers.

A dramatic finale for the students of Istituto Marangoni showing at the London Graduate Fashion Week in June 2011.

Market Research
Chapter 1

Trend Forecasting
Chapter 2

PERSONAL BRIEF

Creative Research
Chapter 3

THEME

Development and Sampling
Chapter 4

CONCEPT

Garment Design and Range Planning
Chapter 5

COLLECTION

Styling
Chapter 6

PRESENTATION

Diffusion and Further Work
Chapter 7

PORTFOLIO

YOUR FINAL COLLECTION

Your degree collection is a major project that will call upon all the skills and abilities you have acquired so far. At the same time it offers great freedom of creative expression and is likely to be the most rewarding experience of your course. You will understandably be feeling both nervous and excited. At the risk of compounding these feelings, you must also recognize that this final stage of your training is a springboard for your career. Consider carefully the implications of the many choices you are about to make. Recognize what your final collection can do for you and engineer this project to serve your own purposes.

WHAT IS THE DIFFERENCE BETWEEN A DEGREE AND A COMMERCIAL COLLECTION?

The project of the final collection is intentionally very similar to that of designing a commercial collection. However, degree and commercial collections are different in two aspects: the nature of the brief and the size of the collection.

Your final collection is a requirement of your curriculum, and as such will be sanctioned by your teaching institution, while a commercial collection can only be validated by the market. Your brief for this project is probably relatively open-ended.

This brief specifies the size of the final collection, which will be significantly smaller than that of most commercial designers. The breadth of a collection allows the emergence of a style through the sequence of outfits, their differences and similarities. While the garments must stand by themselves, each making a statement,

they must also contribute to the overall spirit of the collection. This balance is especially difficult to achieve in a final collection where you must express a broad and innovative vision usually within just four to eight outfits. Each outfit must demonstrate sympathy with the others without being too similar. Together they must exhibit as wide a range of skills as possible.

DEVELOP YOUR STYLE AND YOUR SKILLS

Academia offers a safe environment in which to experiment, and the brief of the final collection gives you artistic licence. This opportunity is unlikely to present itself again in a professional environment, where commercial constraints are always present. Use this freedom to further your own ideas on fashion. Final collections often see the emergence of a personal style and the crystallization of a creative identity.

Your teaching institution also offers resources and technical expertise. At this point you should have an idea of the area of fashion in which you would like to work. The final collection could help you to confirm this – think of it as a dress rehearsal. This practice may also enable you to complete the skill set necessary to succeed in your chosen field. Assess which skills you already have and identify those you need to perfect within the time frame, to ensure that you will be able to produce it to the industry standard. If, for example, you wish to design a lingerie collection you may need to master a number of special techniques such as corsetry, contour wear, lace and surface embellishment, and have access and know-how to operate cover-stitch machinery. Check your department can provide the resources and training you require to succeed.

Line-up from Verena Zeller's collection. (See case study on page 158)

YOUR COLLECTION AND YOUR PORTFOLIO

Your final collection should be useful beyond your degree, not least because it will probably represent the most significant body of work you will have produced by the time you enter the job market. Thus you need to consider how it will fit into your portfolio given the professional direction you would like to pursue. When seeking employment, you must demonstrate that you possess the skills and knowledge required by the position. Your portfolio must show you will be able to contribute to the team you are applying to join by illustrating not only your creativity but also your understanding of the company, its products and target market. Include your final collection in your portfolio *only* if it is relevant to the position you seek. If not, one possibility is to adapt your work by designing a specific **diffusion line** inspired by your final collection. Showing them side by side will demonstrate your creativity as well as your aptitude for designing for different markets. It is a good way to extend the life and use of your final collection.

On the other hand you may consider using your final collection to establish yourself as an independent designer. Sometimes top-end independent boutiques, such as Browns in London (who bought Galliano's 1984 degree collection) or Colette in Paris, will support a freshly graduated student by retailing and promoting their final collection. To successfully launch your label you must not only design an exciting collection, but also establish a viable house style, balancing commerciality with a strong image. This can only be achieved through a thorough understanding of your market.

Line-up from the collection of Kai Ryosuke (See case study on CD).

HOW DOES YOUR INSTITUTION GRADE THE FINAL COLLECTION?

In all likelihood the work involved in developing your final collection will be subject to continuous assessment. There may also be a final assessment involving a jury that could include external academics as well as industry specialists. Methods and criteria for evaluation will vary with each institution. Overall, however, your approach, your development and the execution of your final collection will be assessed, as well as your verbal and visual communication.

Most of the time an explicit and detailed list of assessment criteria and their respective weighting is provided with the project brief, and any further information can be obtained from the course leader. It is your responsibility to understand how your work will be graded, paying attention to both assessment criteria and process.

Continuous assessment allows for *you* to develop a sense of your performance and to adjust your work through the year.

Although jury and final assessment may seem more unpredictable, teaching institutions strive to produce objective and reliable evaluation of student work and provide the jury with well-defined grading criteria. Your grade should not be influenced by a subjective appreciation of what you may be capable of; only the work you produce and submit will be assessed. You should also confirm if external assistance with the production of your collection is allowed. Students from the previous year are a good source of feedback on any practical issues specific to your institution, and you should review their collections in the light of the grade they achieved.

The relative weight of each assessment criterion should help you to manage your time effectively. While designing and producing your collection you will easily lose sight of the conditions you must fulfil to achieve the best grade so, as you familiarize yourself with the assessment process, take notes for future reference. Review those notes regularly to ensure you are on track.

Identify your areas of strength and weakness and be realistic about what you can achieve with the resources available to you. For example, if quality of make ranks prominently in the grading and you intend to include leather in your collection, do you have the skills and machinery necessary to produce garments to a high enough quality? Whenever industry specialists are part of a jury they bring expertise to evaluate the viability of the collections in the real world; their main concern is always the suitability of your collection for its chosen market both commercially and technically. You must ensure that you can design and produce it to this standard.

Assessment usually relies on the documentation and presentation of your development work and eventually on the garments produced for your collection. Each chapter in this book will guide you as to what might be expected for each stage of the process. Overall you should demonstrate very clearly your ownership of the garments and designs presented, and explain the journey you have travelled. Historical and recent trends can be rich and effective sources of inspiration, but simply copying such designs is not acceptable. Within academia plagiarism can lead to suspension or expulsion. Tensions will also arise within a class if students feel their work has been used by others. The originality of your design should be demonstrated by research and development work, presenting a clear evolution from inspiration to finished garment.

Wrapping Up

The brief for the final collection is usually open-ended, so even if your institution does not require you to do so, you will find it helpful to refine it by writing your own personal one. The brief is a reference and a guideline and it focuses the mind on what is to be achieved. By tightening the scope of the original brief you will ensure that your work will fulfil the aims and objectives set by your educational establishment and those you have identified for yourself. The simplest and most effective way to do this is to choose a market, a season, and to select inspiration and influences. The next two chapters will outline the information necessary to make those decisions. Carefully consider these chapters and complement them with your own in-depth research before you contemplate rewriting the brief. Note that in the commercial world designers do not have the luxury of selecting market and season before they start the design process. For them, these are not negotiable constraints.

Your training so far has probably been focused on skills and creativity and less concerned with the commercial reality of fashion. Your final collection is a transition between the comfort of academia and the reality of the work environment. In the real world you will design for a market. When your portfolio is reviewed, you will be asked the target market of your work, so it is imperative to research and understand your clientele.

While backstage is a hive of activity, the last moments before your collection is shown on the catwalk will be charged with excitement and anticipation.

CHAPTER 1
THE DIFFERENT
MARKETS FOR
WOMENSWEAR

The most important parts of any design brief are usually those that refer to the client and this is no different for the final collection. Your design should target a particular woman, one who represents a section of the market. In order to do this successfully you need to develop an in-depth understanding of this woman. Not all teaching institutions require that you carry out this exercise but you will find that it acts as a guide and an inspiration. The notion that this real person could wear your garments can prove very motivating. When you finally show your work and explain whom it is for, your answer will be ready and articulate.

There are various ways to choose and define your client. You may select her because she belongs to a segment of the market you are interested in or, on the contrary, because her needs are not currently properly addressed. You may pick this woman because you have an affinity with her or because she challenges you. To design for her you will need to gain a deep understanding of who she is and what she requires. She will be ever present throughout this project and better company if you like her.

Your research will help you to build a picture of this woman. The information you collect could include socio-economic factors such as cultural heritage, lifestyle, demographics, attitude to fashion and affluence. You are not expected to provide a characterization of your target market as detailed as those provided for market research. However you must be able to describe this woman in a clear, precise way. This can be achieved through a written description of your client in a narrative form. In the fashion industry, however, it is common to build a visual representation of this woman, with images gathered to form a **client board**. This invaluable tool is often displayed in a prime location of the design studio as a reminder and a source of inspiration.

In general your work should be evaluated on its ability to fulfil the requirements of your chosen client. One way to assess this is to compare your work to that of other designers catering for the same woman. In the next section we outline the five main markets for women's fashion and some key specialist areas. You should be able to place your client, and thus your collection, within one of these markets. In highly competitive industries such as fashion, understanding clients and the competition goes hand in hand. Often designers, like retailers, carry out a **comp-shop** – a market study in which information is gathered about the style, quality and price of successful ranges designed by their competitors.

Verena Zeller's approach is to evoke the spirit of a woman. Her approach is not a marketing one but one that provides her inspiration; she shows an understanding of the woman she wants to design for. (See case study on page 158)

TARGET MARKET MARKET SECTOR

Market Sector: Independent Designers Sector.

Competitors: Christopher Kane
Giles Deacon
3.1 Phillip Lim

Target Market: Females between the age group of 25 to 35.
Professional practice in the design or arts industry.
(eg: designers, magazine journalists/editors)
Monthly disposable income of US$ 4000.
Satorial style that is sophisicated, elegant and highly individualistic.
Favourite labels include Chloé, Marni, Jonathan Saunders,
Miu Miu and Christopher Kane.

By specifying a few facts such as job, age, affluence, Bernice Chua clearly identifies the women she intends to design for. She is also aware of the existing labels she will have to compete with. (See case study on CD)

WOMENSWEAR: FIVE FASHION MARKETS

There are five main markets in women's fashion: **haute couture**, **prêt-à-porter** and international luxury brands, designer wear, intermediate and high street. Each has a different style, standard of quality and price range. The evolution of these markets reflects the changing role of fashion in women's lives. The following sections describe each market and give a short historical perspective. Before we begin to look at these markets, though, we need to consider the concept of the diffusion line, as it plays an important role in the historical development of the fashion industry.

Fashion labels must achieve two apparently opposing goals. They must offer wearable and affordable garments yet project a strong and recognizable style. Flamboyant and creative garments favoured by the fashion press are worn by cutting-edge individuals and represent only a small proportion of sales. Designed to attract public attention, they are sometimes referred to as **window dressing** and help to establish and maintain a house style. Perception of quality is often associated with high prices. However, most customers require competitively priced practical clothing. A commercial solution to this dilemma is to complement the original collection with a diffusion line.

While the main collection asserts a strong visual identity, the diffusion line offers garments in a similar but softened style and at a lower price, making the label accessible to a larger portion of the market. The development of the Donna Karan brand is a perfect illustration: in 1985 Donna Karan showed her first women's designer wear collection under the label Donna Karan New York; in 1988 she launched her diffusion label DKNY, in 1990 DKNY Jeans (a denim collection), in 1991 her first signature collection for men, and in 1992 DKNY Men.

HAUTE COUTURE

Haute couture is a French expression that translates literally as 'high sewing'. It evokes luxury and glamour. Haute couture's extraordinary garments are made to measure, often by hand, in the Parisian workshops of **grands couturiers**.

In the seventeenth and eighteenth centuries, fashion was set by the leading ladies at court. Reported in illustrated almanacs, those styles were copied by seamstresses on the instructions of their patrons. Dressmakers had very little artistic licence.

Charles Frederick Worth is credited with the 'invention' of haute couture in 1858, when he opened a workshop in Paris. Worth is considered the first fashion designer as the concept is understood today, proposing fully designed garments and refusing any alteration suggested by his clientele. He established many now-common practices, such as designing collections and showcasing them on live models. Worth became the dictator of fashion in Paris and his business model was quickly imitated. Haute couture was at its peak in 1946 when Paris counted over 100 haute couture houses.

Today, haute couture has become a legally protected label, governed by its union the Chambre Syndicale de la Haute Couture. In order to be awarded this label fashion houses must have a workshop in Paris of at least 15 people ('correspondent' and 'guest' status are available to designers not based in France), present two collections a year to the press and make garments to order with at least one client fitting.

Haute couture garments are cut from the best fabrics and produced with a wide range of sewing techniques, often involving hand finishing (see bridal gown on page 24). They are expensive, with prices sometimes reaching six digits. The regular clientele for haute couture is estimated to be in the region of 200 to 300 women worldwide.

Given this, it is no surprise that the economics of haute couture have proved difficult to sustain and many famous labels no longer produce such collections. Only three correspondents and six guests members showed haute couture collections for Spring/Summer 2010, alongside the ten remaining Parisian names: Adeline André, Anne Valérie Hash, Chanel, Christian Dior, Dominique Sirop, Franck Sorbier, Givenchy, Jean Paul Gaultier, Maurizio Galante and Stéphane Rolland.

Some of these grand couturiers focus solely on haute couture and carry no prêt-à-porter (or ready-to-wear) line, which may explain why their names are less familiar. They tend to run leaner businesses with strict cost control. Their collections are usually smaller and less dramatic than those of the other houses.

The more established names, such as Chanel or Dior, benefit from their haute couture collection in many ways: they have cultivated a clientele that allows their haute couture collection to remain profitable; the know-how and technical skills preserved in the haute couture workshops are useful to the design of the other collections of the house; but mainly the increasingly extravagant and avant-garde haute couture collections are used to promote more commercial lines and contribute to their image and perception.

PRÊT-À-PORTER AND INTERNATIONAL LUXURY BRANDS

Prêt-à-porter refers to the ready-to-wear lines designed by haute couture houses (the French expression literally means 'ready-to-wear'). Prêt-à-porter is the next level down in quality and design from haute couture and is at the very top end of the ready-to-wear market. Like haute couture, it offers a typically French style of fashion and benefits from a powerful heritage with a style and an interpretation of fashion inherited from the founding figure of a particular house. House archives are often used as a rich source of inspiration for new collections.

In 1959 Pierre Cardin caused outrage as the first grand couturier to launch a prêt-à-porter collection. While he designed the collection, its production was outsourced to an industrial facility away from his haute couture workshop. In 1966, another haute couture designer, Yves Saint Laurent followed suit with his 'Rive Gauche' label. This strategy enabled the haute couture houses, under increasing competition from ready-to-wear fashion, to offer high-end designs at more affordable prices while increasing their return on investment.

Since the 1960s most haute couture houses have also run prêt-à-porter lines – usually inspired by the haute couture collections, exploiting their prestige as well as ideas and designs that have been favourably received by the market and promoted by the press. However, they have had to compete with other international luxury brands such as Gucci and Burberry, which started as manufacturers of leather goods and specialized garments respectively. Despite an absence of connection to Paris fashion these brands have achieved international recognition, often thanks to the prestige of these specialist origins.

The high standards and historical lineage of former couture houses, such as Lanvin and Balmain, have kept them at the core of the international luxury market. Increasingly, however, they feel the competition of the most successful designer wear labels.

Produced to a high standard, sold worldwide in house flagship stores and concessions, prêt-à-porter garments are diffusion of haute couture. This ready-to-wear A/W 2010 coat by Jean-Paul Gaultier is clearly related to the one included in his A/W 2009 haute couture collection (opposite page).

DESIGNER WEAR

In the twenty-first century many people associate fashion with designer wear. Designer wear is ready-to-wear produced to a high standard in good-quality materials. Such garments are usually innovative and reflect the unique style of their creator. Designer wear sells at a premium because of the attention to design detail and the relatively small production volumes. Haute couture and prêt-à-porter promote French fashion to an international luxury market. In contrast, designer wear labels have their origins in many parts of the world, often targeting regional markets and covering a wider range of styles and clients.

The life expectancy of designer wear labels varies greatly. They usually have humble beginnings and are initiated by small groups of friends, often with little financial backing. This light structure makes them susceptible to financial difficulties. Until recently they relied on up-market, multi-label boutiques and high-fashion department stores for exposure and sales. However, the development of retail via the internet has modified the rules of the game by allowing them direct access to their markets.

Designer wear labels must have a strong identity and offer a recognizable and successful style over a number of seasons to establish themselves. In order to grow, they must then develop their style to address a larger market without losing their identity. A common strategy is to increase the product range of their collection, eventually developing secondary lines and possibly crossing over into other markets such as menswear or accessories.

Although designer wear labels are commonplace today, they only gained market dominance in the late 70s and early 80s. Their emergence contributed to the establishment of modern national styles of fashion in Italy, the USA, the UK and Japan.

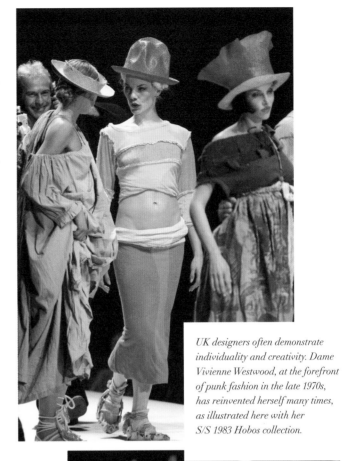

UK designers often demonstrate individuality and creativity. Dame Vivienne Westwood, at the forefront of punk fashion in the late 1970s, has reinvented herself many times, as illustrated here with her S/S 1983 Hobos collection.

The Japanese label Comme des Garçons rose to prominence internationally after making its Paris debut in 1981. Along with other Japanese designers it has relied on the use of black, distressed fabric, asymmetric design and over-sized detailing. This piece from S/S 1989 illustrates some of these characteristics.

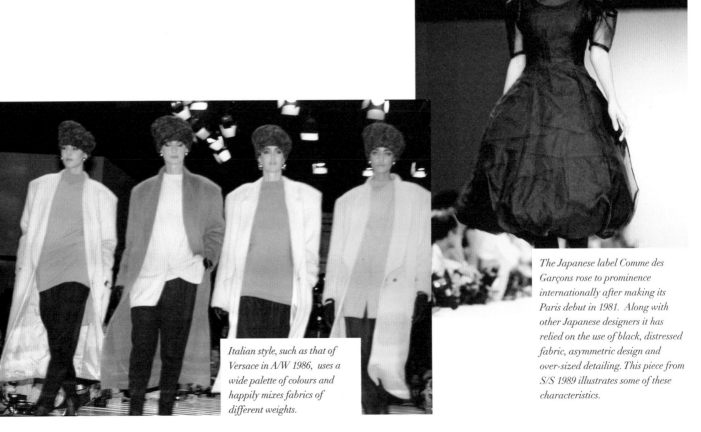

Italian style, such as that of Versace in A/W 1986, uses a wide palette of colours and happily mixes fabrics of different weights.

INTERMEDIATE OR MIDDLE MARKET

The middle market, located between luxury and budget, is difficult to situate precisely. Intermediate fashion is not merely the area defined by two price points; it also implies a conscious attitude to garment purchase – one that favours style and quality over short-term fashion trends.

Although it is usually produced in larger quantities than designer wear, intermediate fashion is not a mass market. It sells because its garments are perceived as value for money: they are manufactured to a good standard, produced in quality fabrics and designed in a style that does not age too quickly. They tend to be targeted at the more affluent woman in her 30s and 40s, and purchased as workwear, for special occasions or as staple garment within a more varied wardrobe. Strongly influenced by social and cultural conventions, intermediate fashion is designed for a national market since occasion wear, in particular, does not cross borders easily.

From left to right: outfits by Emporio Armani A/W 2005, IKKS France A/W 2002 and Ann Taylor S/S 2010. Influenced by developments in international fashion, intermediate labels usually focus on national markets.

HIGH STREET OR MASS MARKET

High street fashion is affordable ready-to-wear designed for a mass market and sold under a brand label. The UK high street has often led the way in fashion retail worldwide. While **fast fashion** and celebrity endorsement have existed in the UK since the 1960s, they became common practices among high street labels in the 1990s. In the same way that grand couturiers produced prêt-à-porter collections, today's designers develop exclusive collections sold under high street labels, lending them their style and prestige.

Fast fashion, the rapid design and delivery of collections to stores, enables high street retailers to satisfy increasingly reactive markets. Real-time stock management, made possible by **EPOS (electronic point of sale)**, provides market intelligence about the styles and colours that sell well and enables retailers to respond quickly to new or micro trends. Collections are designed with high frequency, as often as twice a month, but also rely on **injections** to satisfy client demand. These consist of a single piece or a very limited range which can be designed, produced and delivered in as little as 12 days. Together, these practices not only improve stock management but also spread production and delivery, all of which have financial implications.

Fast fashion and the increased affordability of garments encourage a culture of disposable fashion. In 2006, the Cambridge Institute for Manufacturing estimated that an average of 30 kg of clothes per capita per year was disposed of in the UK. Such an approach to clothing has raised social and environmental concerns. Campaigns to promote ethical and fair trade, as well as the use of organic cotton, have raised public awareness of these issues and prompted the industry to address them. Recycling is increasingly considered as an option by individual designers as well as the high street, and many labels favour organic cotton while new synthetic materials gain market share.

High street fashion and retail in the UK greatly benefitted from the likes of Barbara Hulanicki who, with her shop Biba, imposed the idea of affordable good design, illustrated here by a design from 1968.

Celebrities and famous designers have collaborated with high street labels. Kate Moss, for example, designed several collections for Topshop.

SPECIALIST MARKETS

Too often perceived as unattractive niche markets, specialist areas of fashion, can be very profitable when approached with flair and creativity. There are three underlying reasons to regard a market as 'specialist': first, its clients may have very specific requirements in terms of style or function; secondly, the techniques involved in the production of the goods are specialized; thirdly, the garments are only bought for a special occasion. Each specialist market can be further segmented on the basis of price, style and quality.

Maternity/Plus size

Both maternity wear and plus sizes provide garments for individuals who cannot wear average or standard fits but each market has distinct issues. Women require maternity wear for a few months only and therefore are often reluctant to spend money on such garments, making maternity wear a difficult business proposition. The relative absence of designer wear targeted at plus sizes is more surprising given the potential of this segment. There is, however, an emerging offer for plus sizes in Italy (Cinzia Rocca, Elena Mirò, Marina Rinaldi) and in the USA (Anna Scholz, Lafayette 148) and from international designers. While the silhouette for these markets may be different, designing clothes for them requires as much creativity as designing for any other market.

Mature market

As the western population ages, mature consumers are increasingly influential. In 2009, a Mintel report estimated that in the UK around 80 per cent of national wealth is controlled by those aged over 55. Exposed to a dynamic fashion market, today's older women aspire to look stylish but cuts and styles must be adjusted to suit them.

Club wear

Club wear appeared in the 1990s on the rave scene. Some club wear designers, such as Cyberdog, have proved very creative, using new fabrics, embellishment techniques and quirky silhouettes. Through its music, graphics and fashion, the club scene has had a significant impact on youth culture.

Sportswear

Sportswear plays an important role in streetwear. Tracksuits and trainers first popularized by Bob Marley and the Reggae scene have been embraced by fashion designers and are worn by many away from the pitch. A more recent example of crossover into fashion is surf wear. Other types of sportswear remain pure performance wear, however, and their design demands an in-depth knowledge of their use and function. Often their production also requires specialist material and techniques.

The ever-increasing use of sportswear as casual wear has led to increased investment in its design and to collaboration between fashion designers and sport labels such as Adidas, as illustrated here with a design from 2004.

Accessories

The status of accessories in fashion has significantly changed in the last 20 years. Accessories, like fragrance, represent an affordable way for the consumer to buy into a label. Today most fashion designers have very profitable accessory lines, often organized as a separate collection alongside the main garment lines. In 1997 Louis Vuitton hired Marc Jacobs to design its bags collection and to develop a ready-to-wear line. A great sympathy between the two collections is evident and the garments at times seem to be accessories to the bags.

Bridal

Despite the decline in marriage since the 1970s, brides-to-be continue to spend significant sums on the perfect wedding dress. Indeed, many small fashion ateliers make a living designing and producing such dresses and some designers, such as Vera Wang, have established their name thanks to them. However, it is not a good idea to consider bridalwear for a final collection as its design constraints seriously limit the expression of student creativity and skills.

Lingerie

Lingerie can be a very profitable activity. It is reported that having been on the edge of bankruptcy in the early 90s, Calvin Klein owes its survival in part to the success of its underwear lines. Lingerie and swimwear, like other forms of contour wear, require stretch-fit pattern cutting skills as well as special sewing and cover-stitch machinery.

Knitwear

A few fashion houses such as Missoni specialize in knitwear. Most fashion labels however include knitwear as part of wider collections, particularly Autumn and Winter. Some knitted fabrics, such as jersey, can be cut and sewn using common techniques and equipment and may not actually be considered to be knitwear. Knitted garments produced directly from yarn, fully fashioned knitwear, require specific knitting skills and production facilities, however, and these are not covered by this book.

Like haute couture, high-end bridal gowns are often made to measure. This gown from the Chanel S/S 2010 collection took 1,300 hours to make. Its wide media coverage helped to strengthen Chanel's luxury image.

The house identity of Chantal Thomass will be forever connected with lingerie. This design is from 2004.

Wrapping Up

The business of fashion is complex and its markets are sophisticated. The purpose of this chapter is not to analyse each market in great detail but to make you aware of the importance of choosing one. Some markets, such as haute couture, are focused on a small clientele. In contrast, designer wear covers a multitude of styles and a broad section of the public; it extends from demi-couture, the most expensive of ready-to-wear, to the middle market. Similarly, the high street offers a broad range of styles. Once you have chosen your market, you will need to do more research to narrow your scope and focus on your client.

However choosing a market and understanding your competition is not enough; it can only help you to understand what is current, what works and sells today. As a designer you must design today what people will wear tomorrow.

Missoni, originally a family knitwear company, known for the colourful pattern of its material – such as the one in this 2005 design – is now a fashion empire branching into many areas, including hotels.

CHAPTER 2
FASHION IN TIME

You are probably familiar with this scenario: summer arrives and at long last coats and woollens are discarded and replaced by exciting new summer clothes. New collections are in the shops and commentators declare an 80s revival. Shoulders and sleeves are big. Earthy neutrals compete with vibrant pink, blue and golden yellows. Accessories and jewellery are large and colourful. A visit to a few shops reveals that this is just what is on the racks at the moment and soon you start noticing people wearing this new style.

Let's pause and think about this. How and why do styles vary from one season to the next? Why are only a few identical fashion colours available in shops? How did the 80s' big shoulders, so despised in the 90s, manage to make a comeback and why are they featured in so many collections?

This chapter explains the ways in which time affects garment designs, and how the industry manages the constant evolution of fashion. It also provides a brief overview of how the fashion industry operates. This is vital for anyone seeking employment in this sector. Furthermore, some aspects of its organization have direct consequences for the way you should approach your final collection. Like professional designers, fashion students must design significantly ahead of their markets and anticipate the directions these markets will take to ensure that their work is in tune with the times and received with enthusiasm. To be successful, fashion collections should neither feel tired nor be overly avant-garde. They must be needed and exciting.

The most noticeable effect of time on fashion is that of the seasons. As winter follows summer, garments must be adapted to provide comfort and protection. Fashion students should mention in their brief the season for which their collection is intended, and take into account any seasonal design constraints.

To deliver garments in time each season, the industry has established a demanding calendar. The industrial production of garments, now often carried out abroad, has significantly decreased production costs but the process of manufacturing and delivering these garments to the marketplace is lengthy. Consequently, designers in the industry must design a year ahead of retail. Fashion students must work even more in advance of the selling season as academic and industry calendars are not in sync.

A number of tools and techniques are available to help designers anticipate the direction fashion markets will take, and the last section of this chapter will look at the work of **trend forecasters**, with an example provided by Mudpie, the largest UK-based trend forecast company.

FASHION SEASONS

The primary function of clothing is to protect the body from the elements. To provide comfort during summer and winter extremes, garments are produced in different qualities and weights of material as well as different colours; light colours reflect heat and so are worn in summer whilst dark ones absorb it and consequently are more suited to winter. The fashion industry is organized around these seasonal requirements and addresses them with Spring/Summer (S/S) and Autumn (Fall)/Winter (A/W) collections, delivered to retail shops from the end of January and the end of August respectively. Globally the industry follows the northern hemisphere calendar and garments sold in the southern hemisphere – which accounts for only 10 per cent of the world's population – are either designed locally or follow international fashion with a six-month delay.

In most climates, winter weather requires larger garments worn in multiple layers and produced in warmer materials, often in expensive yarns. This results in large and costly A/W collections. Over the last 20 years, an increasing number of labels offer 'Pre-Fall' collections in an attempt to spread manufacture and delivery of garments over time, thereby smoothing cash flow. These collections, in shops from the end of June, are made in materials of intermediate weight and allow for a more gradual transition to winter. A similar organization is emerging with S/S collections. Milan having set a trend, professional trade fairs (or **salons**) are now organized twice a year, to sell 'pre-collections'.

Some fashion labels have developed seasonal niche markets. Haute couture and top luxury labels, for example, design cruise collections available in November when their affluent clientele escapes to sunny destinations. As winter holidays have become more affordable, resort wear collections are also offered by the middle market.

When considering your final collection brief you must pick a season and fully assess the impact it will have on your garments. You will need to make coherent choices of colour, material and garment types. Such constraints, however, can also present opportunities for designers, who may extend the life of some of their designs by changing the weight and colours of their fabrics to adapt them for another season.

These two Prada outfits, one from A/W 2007 and the other from S/S 2006, illustrate some of the usual and traditional differences in fabric weight and colour between winter and summer.

Cruise and pre-collections often achieve high volumes of sales, in part because an absence of media reporting allows focus on commercial pieces. This outfit is typical of the commerciality of the Viktor & Rolf cruise 2011 collection, unlike some of their more extreme designs (see page 85).

THE DESIGN-TO-RETAIL CYCLE

Students designing and producing a degree collection within an academic environment have little opportunity to learn how orders are taken, produced and delivered in the real world – knowledge that is critical when working or seeking employment. Designers must never forget that their work does not end with design; their success depends on each of the stages up to, and including, retail. Experience gained away from the design studio is often mentioned to explain the success of some designers: Tom Ford's spell in retail or Alexander McQueen's in tailoring, for example.

The length of the design-to-retail cycle as followed in industry today explains why the design of a collection must get underway in advance. The fashion industry works a year forward and it is in this context that portfolios and collections are viewed. If your collection fits with the fashion currently in the shops it will, in fact, be considered over a year old. This will be obvious to anyone working in the industry and will fail to impress them.

The cycle presented here is typical of the prêt-à-porter and designer wear market. Haute couture and the high street present some variations, mentioned later. This cycle can be broken into four stages: design, sales, production and delivery to clients.

DESIGN

Fashion designers must deliver a minimum of two, usually four, and often more, collections a year. To produce them on time the design process usually starts a year ahead of retail. This process usually begins with an analysis carried out by the sales and production teams of the previous collection's performance. It provides an objective evaluation of the house style and range plan which can be used when designing the next collection.

As the creative process unfolds, designers present their initial ideas to the sales and communication teams to discuss the relevance of the chosen direction and prepare styling and communication. Later on, when **toiles** have been completed and fabrics selected, the production team checks the feasibility and the cost of the designs. Once this is done, the sales team will confirm the commercial viability of each garment based on its production cost and its anticipated retail price. This process may lead to changes in cut or material or even the decision to remove the garment from the collection.

Throughout the design stage, therefore, the creative team relies on the rest of the business to guide some of their choices. Fashion students will not have the benefit of such inputs and academic staff cannot be expected to be knowledgeable and fully up-to-date with all markets. It is therefore vital that students thoroughly research their market before starting to design their collection.

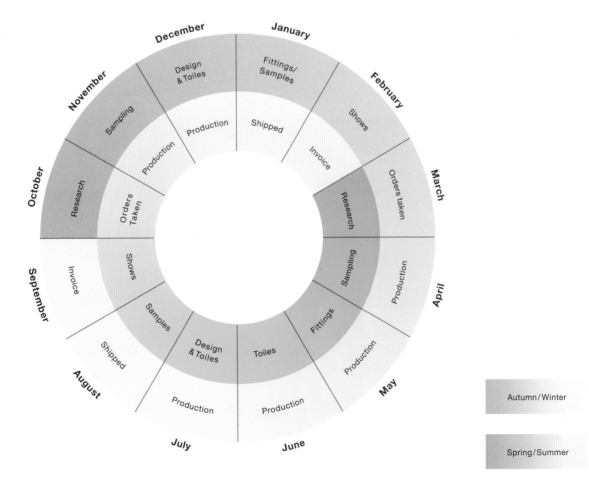

SALES

The process by which sales take place in fashion has been ritualized and follows a strict and demanding calendar. The major Fashion Weeks held in Milan, London, Paris and New York are scheduled twice a year – spring and autumn – for women's ready-to-wear; and, for haute couture, they take place in Paris in winter and summer. International buyers, models and designers will travel from capital to capital in the business of buying and selling fashion.

Buyers are offered different ways to view collections and place orders. Catwalk shows focus on attracting media and public attention; they play a vital role in the communication of fashion houses through the spectacle and images they offer. After a show, buyers can view the garments again in salons, where they then book their orders. Putting on a catwalk show is expensive and often collections are presented only in salons. (Fashion students should enjoy and make the most of their degree show as showing on a catwalk is in fact a relatively rare opportunity.) Salon presentations are usually organized as trade fairs, gathering together a number of labels. One of the best known is the Salon International du Prêt à Porter, which takes place in Paris every January and September.

By the beginning of the twenty-first century Fashion Weeks have multiplied around the world, offering a market place for local designers and buyers who cannot afford to travel to the international fashion centres.

Some labels have started to use the internet to communicate with their markets and clientele. Shows are streamed online, sometimes in real time, and fashion designers may have their own boutique on the net. Innovative internet retail techniques such as **crowd funding**, connecting the public with designer to finance directly the production of a collection, may change the way fashion is sold. Internet-based communication and retail strategies are reasonably inexpensive and easy to put in place and should be considered by students wishing to retail their final collections.

PRODUCTION

Garment production is almost always outsourced to a large and varied range of production or **CMT (Cut, Make and Trim)** facilities available worldwide. Outsourcing requires effective collaboration between the in-house production manager and the CMT factory to ensure garments are delivered in the required quality and on time.

Once all the orders for the season have been taken they are compiled and may be confirmed with the buyers. Often there is a minimum batch size required for factory production and if this volume is not achieved the order may be cancelled or produced in-house.

The production manager must confirm the availability of fabric and source and order the trims in the correct colours, all to be delivered to the factory. For each style, patterns must be graded in the usual four sizes, S, M, L, XL, and labels with global sales must adjust cuts to fit the average body proportions of customers in the different world markets where the collection has been sold.

Before the order (or **docket**) is finally placed for production, the factory must produce a **sealed sample** for each style. The sample demonstrates the quality that the factory will commit to producing, and it must be approved by the designer.

Following the example of Thierry Mugler in the 1980s, Alexander McQueen's dramatic presentation of his collections in the 1990s generated a huge amount of press. For his 1998 Joan of Arc Collection he set the stage ablaze.

DELIVERY TO RETAIL

Delivery to retail is organized according to the periodicity of the collection and is usually staggered over a period of up to three months. The sequence and size of each delivery is organized with the client so that coherent stories of merchandise are available to be shown at retail. A **story** is a group of coordinated separates that can be merchandised in a coherent way on the shop floor. This delivery schedule obviously requires careful planning at production level to ensure a smooth flow in and out of production to shipping. By the time a collection is being delivered, the following season's collection is being shown and ordered.

VARIATIONS IN OTHER MARKETS

This design-to-retail cycle is very similar in most fashion markets; however production in haute couture and sales in high street fashion are organized slightly differently.

Haute couture garments are produced to order and with individual fittings in the house workshop, so there is no wholesale or outsourcing of production. The time lag between catwalk show and wear is also shorter; collections are shown in early July for A/W and in late January for S/S. Collections are presented in private salons or catwalk shows with high production values.

One of the characteristics of high street fashion is that the same company generally controls both design and retail. The design studio at headquarters may be removed from the workshop part of a production facility. The low cost of garments given the volume of production means the toiling stage is often skipped and collections are edited with garments made in their final fabric. High street does not wholesale to independent boutiques, so 'sales' is very much an internal process that allocates styles to shops.

The high street organizes design and production in accordance with the life cycle of the garment in store. Production of staple clothes, for example, is organized well in advance, and delivery is regular as volumes change little from one season to the next. On the other hand, the production cycle for fast fashion items, as explained in the previous chapter, is much shorter.

Presentation and merchandising at retail also plays an important role in the success of a label.

EXAMPLE OF AN ANNUAL FASHION CALENDAR

Presentation	Location and market	Season	Delivered from
Jan 25 – 28	Paris – haute couture	S/S	Mid-March same year
Feb 11 – 18	New York – ready-to-wear	A/W	August same year
Feb 19 – 24	London – ready-to-wear	A/W	August same year
Feb 24 – Mar 3	Milan – ready-to-wear	A/W	August same year
Mar 2 – 10	Paris – ready-to-wear	A/W	August same year
April	Various locations – ready-to-wear	Cruise	November same year
May 18 – Jun 18	Milan and various locations – ready-to-wear	Pre-Spring	November same year
Jul 5 – 8	Paris – haute couture	A/W	September same year
Sep 9 –16	New York – ready-to-wear	S/S	January following year
Sep 17– 22	London – ready-to-wear	S/S	January following year
Sep 22 – 29	Milan – ready-to-wear	S/S	January following year
Sep 28 – Oct 7	Paris – ready-to-wear	S/S	January following year
Nov 16 – Dec 16	Milan and various locations – ready-to-wear	Pre-Fall	June following year

ACADEMIC VERSUS INDUSTRY TIME CYCLES

Working a year ahead is second nature to creative people in fashion; those same people will review your portfolio and may grade your final collection. Like them you must design forward. There is a further twist, however: the academic calendar is not synchronized with that of the industry. Students show their final collection in May or June and usually interview from August. This means that a student Spring/Summer final collection must be four months ahead of the industry and a total of sixteen months in advance of retail; an Autumn/Winter final collection must be eight months ahead of the industry and a total of twenty months in advance of retail.

Fashion Weeks generate wide media coverage and front-row seating is reserved for the leading fashion press.

TRENDS IN FASHION

Our relationship with clothes, what we express through them and what we find attractive, changes all the time. Women freely select from garments on offer; how they coordinate and wear them is also a personal decision. These individual styles, however, are often shared by a group of women and may be said to be the *fashion* amongst them. 'Fashion is a social agreement, the result of a consensus of a large group of people' (Stella Blum).

The clothes on offer, like the ones we desire and wear, are affected by developments in the fashion industry but also by socio-economic factors and events across the world. A convergence in these influences may lead to the emergence of a style that becomes popular and dominant: a fashion or a trend. This process is central to fashion. Understanding why people choose to wear certain garments and what influences fashion more broadly is the first step towards identifying the direction in which it may evolve. It is an invaluable skill for fashion designers.

WHAT INFLUENCES FASHION?

A garment may be described by three main characteristics: its *technical make-up*, the techniques and technologies necessary to make it; its *functionality*, the practical purpose it fulfils; and its *aesthetics*, the way it fits into the current notion of beauty. The relationship between these three characteristics is complex and at the heart of design.

Technological progress plays an important role in the development of fashion as it helps to make certain designs possible. The colour purple, for example, became very fashionable in the 1860s following the discovery by William Perkin of the first synthetic dye (mauveine); until that time its natural dye made this colour prohibitively expensive. Similarly, textile innovation plays a major role. The tight-fitting garments so fashionable in the 1980s, for example, were made possible by the earlier invention of Spandex (elastane), a material which recovers its original shape after being stretched.

The functional requirement of apparel changes with context and over time; it is influenced by a wide range of factors such as societal developments, social conventions and practical constraints. Changes in the practical functions of certain types of apparel will lead to new designs and, in turn, to the emergence of new aesthetics. At the beginning of the twentieth century, for example, the desire or necessity for women to lead more physically active lives eventually led to the demise of corsets and heavy garments. The new silhouette this promoted was controversial at the time; it blurred the lines between social classes and was seen as unflattering. However the demand for more practical, comfortable garments led to new designs and eventually to an appreciation of this silhouette.

Finally, the aesthetics of fashion, like the notion of what constitutes beauty generally, change over time, often influenced by the wider cultural context. There may be a convergence in the themes and sensitivities expressed in different creative fields, such as the fine arts, architecture, industrial design, and film and television as well as fashion. Together they contribute to the development of a modern aesthetic, which in turn influences both fashion designers and their clients. While some designers deny being influenced by trends, they cannot fail to be affected by their overall cultural environment. The miniskirt was designed by different people in different places, but at the same time: it is representative of an era – the 1960s.

Overall a broad range of factors can affect the evolution of fashion, from the state of the economy (the utilitarian fashion of Edward Molyneux post WWII) to gender politics (the miniskirt), from youth movements (the Punks in the 1970s) to the ubiquitous presence of celebrity in the media.

Sienna Miller's personal style promoted Boho Chic. Her repeated presence in the media following her engagement to Jude Law in 2004 gave the trend exposure and appeal.

1940s
UNKNOWN DESIGNER

1960s
AQUAMARINE

1930s
BURBERRY

1950s
UNKNOWN DESIGNER

**1970s
CHRISTIAN DIOR**

**1990s
RALPH LAUREN**

**1980s
ANTONY PRICE**

The evolution of the water-proof coat, a garment that fulfills a well-defined function, has been quite dramatic, adjusting for changing aesthetics and silhouettes.

FASHION TRENDS

A fashion trend is the prevailing style of garment that people within a group adopt at one point in time. For example, Dior's late 1940s 'New Look', with its nipped-in waist and full skirt, was a trend that remained popular in Europe and America well into the 1950s.

While it is relatively easy to identify the popular silhouettes of past fashion, the study of current fashion and emerging trends often requires the deconstruction of fashion styles into elements of design: the details that contribute to a style and by which it is described, for example the use of a colour palette, the level of a hemline, the shoulder line and so on. These details may eventually constitute trends that, in turn, can lead to the establishment of an overall look or silhouette if an aesthetic coherence links those elements of design together.

Fashion trends may be short-lived or long-lived. Before fast fashion they tended to last at least a season, but today the high street identifies and responds to much shorter trends, typically lasting only a few weeks. Other trends are much longer, lasting almost a decade in the case of the hipster and low-rise fashion of the 1990s, for example. Trends emerge, peak and eventually lose momentum. They may disappear completely or remain dormant until a later resurgence. Fashion has gained in complexity with globalization, ease of access and the precise segmentation of markets and trends increasingly coexist and overlap.

The use of curved shapes in the late 1950s by world-renowned architect Oscar Niemeyer redirected International Style architecture, away from straight lines, towards organic shapes. Compounded by the space conquest and new plastic technologies it led to the emergence of a futurist/space trend which had a great impact on all decorative arts of the 1960s and early 1970s.

MECHANISMS OF TREND FORMATION IN FASHION

The business of trend analysis has identified a variety of reasons that explain why fashion styles may become successful, and it has produced two distinct theories used to explain the emergence of past trends – **trickle-down** and **bubble-up**.

The trickle-down theory best explains fashion in the second half of the nineteenth and first half of the twentieth centuries. It illustrates an elitist approach to fashion where designers define an aesthetic and a must-have fashion that is eventually emulated by the wider population. In short, this model describes how the fashion industry may subtly coerce people into adopting a style.

The bubble-up theory describes the influence of popular culture on fashion, often seen in the second half of the twentieth century, when a fashion style would emerge in the street (e.g. Teddy Boys, Punk, Hip-Hop…). Styles originally worn by a small group of people, often adopted as a political statement, or popular on the music scene, were adopted by a wider population, often after they had gained visibility in the media. On a few occasions they even inspired haute couture designers. This theory highlights the accepted notion that trends cannot emerge without the endorsement of the people who wear the clothes.

In the twenty-first century the weight of the elite and the influence of the street have balanced out and it may be more useful today to consider cross-pollination between different fashion participants, a theory sometimes called **trickle-across**.

These theories describe the increasing attractiveness of a style as it gains popularity and exposure; ironically its appeal starts to wear off when the style becomes mainstream and it eventually goes out of fashion. The same key participants, sometimes in different guise, are always present in the establishment of a trend. First, there are the individuals at the origin of the style, perhaps designers, youth movements or music artists. They are the Leading Edge, the first people to adopt the style and often regarded as outrageous by the rest of the population. To become popular the style must then be adopted by a second group, the Trend Setters. They may be film stars, musicians, political activists or even gang leaders, but all are high-profile and influential individuals who are emulated. Eventually, the style may be adopted by a larger portion of the population as it becomes mainstream: the third and final group. Within that group, as the trend gains momentum we distinguish between Early Adopters and Late Adopters as some people seem to be more sensitive to new trends than others. This highlights the fact that familiarity with a style over a period of time seems to make it more acceptable. Clearly our perception of a style is easily influenced and changes with time.

Youth movements have significantly influenced fashion in the second half of the twentieth century. Hip-hop musicians wear heavy chain jewellery in remembrance of their slave heritage. Increase in the popularity of their music in the late 1980s inspired Chanel to design, in Autumn 1991, a collection labelled Hip-Hop.

TRENDS IN COLOUR

Colour is an important component of design and is also subject to trends; after an extended period of popularity a colour that once was exciting may become boring. Every year the textile industry tries to forecast which colours will be popular, however every year some of these colours do not sell and end up dominating the discounted stocks in sales. The production of this unsold stock comes at a cost to the industry, the consumer and the environment. Avoiding this is the mission of **colour forecasting** (part of the trend forecasting industry); it is not an easy task.

The selection of colours in which garments are offered at retail is a complex process. Once fashion companies have taken orders from retail they must quickly organize production and order fabrics and trims in the required colours; not all colours, however, are carried in stock. Over-dyeing, the dyeing of a whole piece of cloth from **grey state**, is a possible solution for some fabrics, but it does not work on all fibres. Manufacture of fabric often requires the dying of yarn before it is woven, a process that extends the time delay between choice of colour and availability of stock.

The only solution is for the textile industry to anticipate the market and dye yarn and fabric ahead of orders, relying on a forecast of fashion colours. The work involved to publish such forecast reports usually takes six months. Available two years before delivery of garments to the retail market, these reports are the basis on which fabrics manufacturers choose the colours they will dye their yarn. A year before the retail of garments, as designers start working on the design of their collection, manufacturers reveal their stock colours at major textile shows such as Première Vision. Fashion designers, aware of the palette proposed to the market, will in turn choose their fashion colours. Again, the choice of garment colours proposed by designers to retail will influence the decision made by the wholesale buyers. Overall the selection of the colours that will eventually be available at retail depends on a series of choices informed in part by what the previous actors in the cycle have decided. For this reason the original colour forecast is sometimes viewed as a self-fulfilling prophecy, as no one who chooses fashion colours can benefit from stepping too far away from it. This is not entirely true as some of the forecasted colours do not sell despite being 'promoted' by this selection process.

Forecasting seasonal colours like forecasting any other trend is not an exact science; it is a difficult art on which various sections of the fashion industry rely, especially those needing mainstream appeal. Depending on the market they target, designers may choose to rely on explicit trend forecasts, or they may prefer to trust their own intuition. Sometimes they seek to cultivate an individual identity away from fads. In any case, understanding the techniques used by trend forecasters will assist in generating a collection in tune with the times.

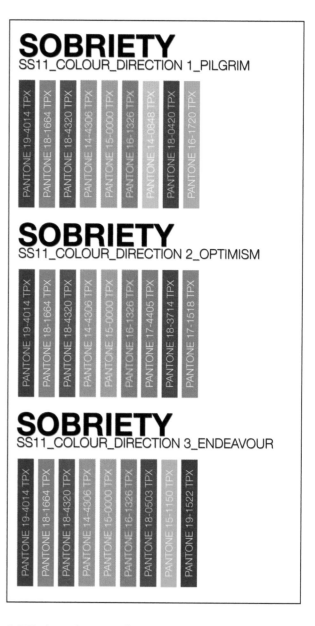

In 2009, the trend service Mudpie forecasted a colour palette for S/S 2011 called 'Sobriety', proposing three variations. Independent work from renowned UK designers Christopher Kane, Giles Deacon and Erdem for S/S 2011 show different interpretations of these palettes.

TREND FORECASTING

Trend forecasting is carried out by independent agencies that research and analyse world events, cultural and social developments, and consumer and fashion markets in order to produce reports and forecasts on the development of trends. Such forecasts are valuable not only to designers but also retailers, buyers, merchandisers and marketing agencies dealing with a number of consumer goods.

While market research observes consumers' current behaviour, trend forecasting is interested in what they will do *tomorrow*: that is, in 12 to 30 months' time. It tries to characterize the fashion people will want in the future. This cannot be achieved by directly questioning consumers, as their answers are bound to reflect their current tastes. Trend forecasting analyses how their behaviour will change and how aesthetics may develop. It identifies and analyses emerging and leading-edge styles that may develop into trends and become mainstream. This requires the analytical interpretation of a wide array of information; it is not a creative activity but it often employs trained fashion designers who can contribute their knowledge and understanding of fashion.

AN INTERVIEW WITH MUDPIE

Founded in 1992 by CEO Fiona Jenvey, Mudpie is one of the most dynamic and widely used trend services in the market and is considered a thought leader in the industry today. With 20 years of industry experience, Mudpie offers their thousands of international users the benefit of their online and printed trend books and creative services. Mudpie is the only online trend forecasting service with an on-site design studio, enabling it to produce accurate, commercial and trend-led information for creative businesses. Many well-known brands also use its consultancy services.

Services are also popular with students, who value Mudpie's creative and collaborative approach. Many have experienced this either as users, interns or as part of their social networking initiatives.

As with all trend services, Mudpie works alongside an international network of contributors, journalists, photographers and trend hunters, all dedicated to providing it with global insight and original ideas.

Sarah Wade, Mpdclick's Managing Editor, discusses Mudpie's approach.

What are the services that you offer?
Mudpie offers trend information to the creative industries. Our three key services are our range of printed seasonal trend books, our online trend service, mpdclick.com, and our strategic creative solutions offered within our consultancy business.

Can you tell us more about trend books?
Mudpie provide a complete selection of trend books each season. Each book includes seasonal background information on the cultural events, products and people that have inspired the various trends. Following this, a full Pantone-referenced, fabric-swatched palette provides a hands-on look at how seasonal colours translate onto fabric. Trends are then conveyed in sets of fully coloured garment designs, each set displayed as a capsule collection. Finally, a CD contains editable versions of the book's garments, graphics and prints. The six trend book titles each cater for a separate market segment: baby, kids,

PARIS_A/W 11/12_CHRISTIAN DIOR_DETAILS, ACCESSORIES & FOOTWEAR

Date: 08/03/2011

◄‖ Add a link to this report to 'My Bookmarks' » | See all 53 pictures »

christian dior_ paris (fra)_a/w 11/12_female_details, accessories & footwear

© christian dior   © christian dior   © christian dior   © christian dior   © christian dior

◄‖ Add to folder   ◄‖ Add to folder   ◄‖ Add to folder   ◄‖ Add to folder   ◄‖ Add to folder
Download jpg   Download jpg   Download jpg   Download jpg   Download jpg

See all 53 pictures

male and female apparel, active wear and print and pattern. The trend books are published two years ahead of the selling season.

What is available on mpdclick.com?

Season on season, Mpdclick takes its users on a chronological guide through in-depth trend research and development, keeping subscribers updated. Mpdclick's blog, the *Trend Journal*, documents the team's initial findings, forming the basis of forecasted trends two years ahead of season. Mpdclick follows these seeds of thought in its dedicated Trend Research area, providing analysis into key events and influences through its bi-monthly interactive magazine and online reports. Here, three seasonal trends are named for the first time.

Ambient trend-led colour palettes are then published two years ahead of real time when the design process begins. Textile, interior materials, print and graphics inspiration is then published in the months leading up to the forecast conclusion, 18 months ahead of real time. Finally, garment, accessory and footwear inspiration, complete with

fully editable and downloadable range plans and graphic designs, is published for each trend, gender and age group. Subscribers are then provided with a complete, accurate overview of what the forecasted trends for each season will look like.

Users of Mpdclick also benefit from seasonal coverage from the worlds of designer ready-to-wear, haute couture, trade fair and retail. Spanning fashion, interiors and sports, Mpdclick's inspirational image galleries and usable design tools aid all areas of global creative businesses.

Finally, besides Mpdclick, Mudpie also provides resources accessible to students via its online Student Resource Area and education group on social networking platform LinkedIn.

How does consultancy for specific clients work?
Mudpie's consultancy provides bespoke design solutions, created for brands by trend-led designers. An initial consultation establishes the requirements of the customer and a clear brief is agreed. Project mood boards are created to fit with the customer's product and market level. Colour palettes are also decided along with the main themes and trends the client wishes to follow. Often colours will be adapted from the palettes used in Mudpie's trend books to fit the products and design then begins.

Can you talk us through your forecast for A/W 2011–12?
Now that consumer decadence has come to an end, 'The New Equilibrium' creates a stable path for future growth, bringing renewed opportunities for brands; the challenge for retailers is to think the unthinkable, accepting that the 'consumer age' has entered a new phase. 'Consideration' is a key consumer trend of the decade. Today's customer, no longer afraid of reality, is adapting to a new model for living based on an alternative future that combines science and technology with social cohesion and collective influence. A new globally connected peer-to-peer culture has evolved, producing a refreshed sense of community. As the environment continues as the defining issue of our age, we are set for

an energy revolution and a plan of action with longevity firmly in mind. Certainly brands and retailers must adapt to emerging patterns of consumption, utilizing design to deliver originality, quality and transparency through all levels of the supply chain.

A/W 2011–12 explores an instinct for harmony and stability. From the umbrella trend 'The New Equilibrium', Mudpie develops three commercial design trends. 'Synergy' (illustrated below) considers a new lifestyle model of pragmatism, simplicity and community, mirrored by more discerning consumer tastes for quality and value. The socio-ecological ideology of Scandinavia represents a new model for modern living. In contrast, 'Primal' (illustrated overleaf) reflects primitive instincts for survival and values ancestral practices and customs, while celebration of the natural elements provides optimism in the face of adversity. Finally, in 'Innovate' (illustrated opposite) we calculate that science will provide the ultimate technological solution.

SOME LESSONS FROM TREND FORECASTING

Fashion students must recognize the importance of trends in fashion and the ways in which these affect the different markets. Middle market and high street collections are the main users of trend forecasting as they try to appeal to a wide section of the population; their commercial success is clearly affected by fashion trends. This also applies to most diffusion lines, which try to extend the market reach of the original labels. While trends may be less important in other fashion markets that value identity and differentiation, the concepts and techniques drawn from the practice of trend forecasting invariably help to strengthen a designer's 'intuition' or prescience.

Fashion is subject to a wide range of influences, and styles trickle across different markets. Trend forecasters must maintain a well-informed and broad perspective in order to interpret the meaning and significance of recent developments in fashion and detect emerging trends. Similarly, designers must not lose sight of what happens in the broader context while also cultivating an in-depth understanding of their own markets.

Trend forecasters must be open minded and objective. They must avoid being influenced by their own taste and preferences and always be receptive to the next influence. Fashion designers, on the other hand, must also cultivate their own style and identity.

To correctly analyse the information they have gathered, trend forecasters must assess its impact, taking into account how often it is likely to be viewed. The impact of a feature will vary according to whether it is published in *Vogue*, for example, or on a relatively unknown blog unlikely to be noticed; this appreciation however must be balanced by the rate of occurrences of a similar feature; if often repeated it may signal the emergence of a trend not yet embraced by a leading publication.

Trend forecasters often identify trends and argue their forecasts by deconstructing designs to highlight recurrent themes and details. They may also pick apart aspects of a current trend to identify how it is likely to evolve and which aspects may increase or decrease in importance in the future. Analysing a design through deconstruction can be very useful to any designer.

Once a number of emerging styles have been identified, trend forecasters must be able to produce a short list of those that will be influential. This short list can be established either through selection or by elimination. Trend forecasters eliminate styles which they feel are not yet acceptable to the market. Designers should regularly consider the acceptability of their design — whether it will be understood and appeal at the current stage in the evolution of aesthetics — and be able to edit their work accordingly.

Wrapping Up

This chapter has highlighted the central role that time plays in fashion. By definition any fashion is 'in' for a limited period of time and it can age quickly. The fashion industry constantly promotes new styles, however only a few are successful. Their success depends not only on the way they answer clients' requirements but also how the aesthetics they promote resonate with current tastes. Because of the logistical constraints of industrial production, there is almost a year's delay between design and retail of garments. But being forward and creative does not give licence for haphazard designs; designers must ensure their work is fresh and new but also accessible. Fashion students are often given license to be creative and investigate their artistic identity. In such cases their final collection may not need to adhere to trend forecasts but, under no circumstances, can it appear passé.

Now that you have considered the different women's fashion markets you may address, and have understood that your garments must be designed forward (16 months for S/S collections and 20 months for A/W) and for a specific season, you are ready to refine the brief of your collection and articulate the constraints you choose to work with. This means placing yourself in conditions similar to those of a commercial designer. On the other hand, you may be concerned about setting too many constraints early on. How and when you finalize your own brief is your choice; do it when it best suits you. Some students choose to wait and do it after completing their creative research (see Chapter 3).

Do not forget, however, that limiting the field of your creativity will focus your attention and energy. By keeping your options open you have the possibility of backtracking but also run the risk of seriously upsetting your timetable; do not forget your deadlines.

Fashion is, in its essence, trend. Some garment designs, however, are timeless and difficult to date. These two garments for example have been designed twenty years apart, the first by Yohji Yamamoto for A/W 2009, the second by Calvin Klein in 1989.

FINALIZING YOUR PERSONAL BRIEF

The designer's brief is an important tool in the creative industry. It defines what the designer must achieve by specifying the purpose of his or her designs as well as their constraints. The brief for the design of a uniform, for example, may mention practical requirements of this garment relating to its function and the level of comfort it must provide, but also describe the corporate image it must project. A thorough and well-thought-out brief is essential to produce the best design and any omission may lead to a product that is unfit for purpose.

Final collection briefs are usually broad and flexible so as to give students a level of freedom. Even if you are not required to do so, writing a personal brief, restricting the scope of the project, always proves useful as it helps to focus attention and creativity. The absence of a specific brief may lead to the design of a collection of vague commercial standing. Writing a personal brief will not only help you to stay on track during its design but will also assist you during the creative stage. Knowing and understanding the purpose of your work and who will wear your garments can only help in their design. Such a brief must be formulated with great care, though, as its purpose is not to be abandoned later on.

As long as you respect the framework set by your teaching institution, you can write your own personal one in any way you like. Before you do so, you may want to review some of the considerations mentioned so far. Overall, you must be both ambitious and realistic about what can be achieved:

Review the constraints and requirements set by your teaching institution, paying attention to the original brief and to the criteria and process of grading the final collection

Consider what you want to achieve in terms of acquisition of skills and creative development

Think about your ambitions beyond your final academic year and the role your collection will play in your portfolio and in the context of a job search

Acknowledge the practical constraints you must manage in order to achieve those aims. This includes an honest estimation of what you can already do, what you will be able to learn and the support you can expect.

Ideally you should compile a list of your strengths and weaknesses that covers:

Your understanding of the market you have chosen and your appreciation of its trends

The technical skills and abilities required to produce such a collection to industry standards

The time this may require against your timetable

Access to the necessary material and equipment

The financial cost of producing your collection

The resources available for presentation and styling, whether in terms of a catwalk show or a studio and editorial photo shoot

In the industry, commercial constraints are not negotiable; your personal brief must mirror those restrictions and mention the market and the season for which your collection is intended. In addition to the five markets for women's fashion (see p. 17) there are many interesting niche markets you could consider. Remember that the choice of season will affect how forward your collection must be.

You may intend a more specific purpose for your garments or have considered a particular way in which to approach their design, for example you may want to design them with the environment in mind by being economical with your use of fabric or by using organic and recycled material. These early and supplementary constraints could also be included in your brief.

Overall make sure that your brief strikes a suitable balance between reliance on your strengths – skills on which you can capitalize – and areas in which you are not so strong but you wish to develop as they may affect your early career development. Remember that you need to further investigate the overview given in Chapters 1 and 2 once you have chosen your market and season.

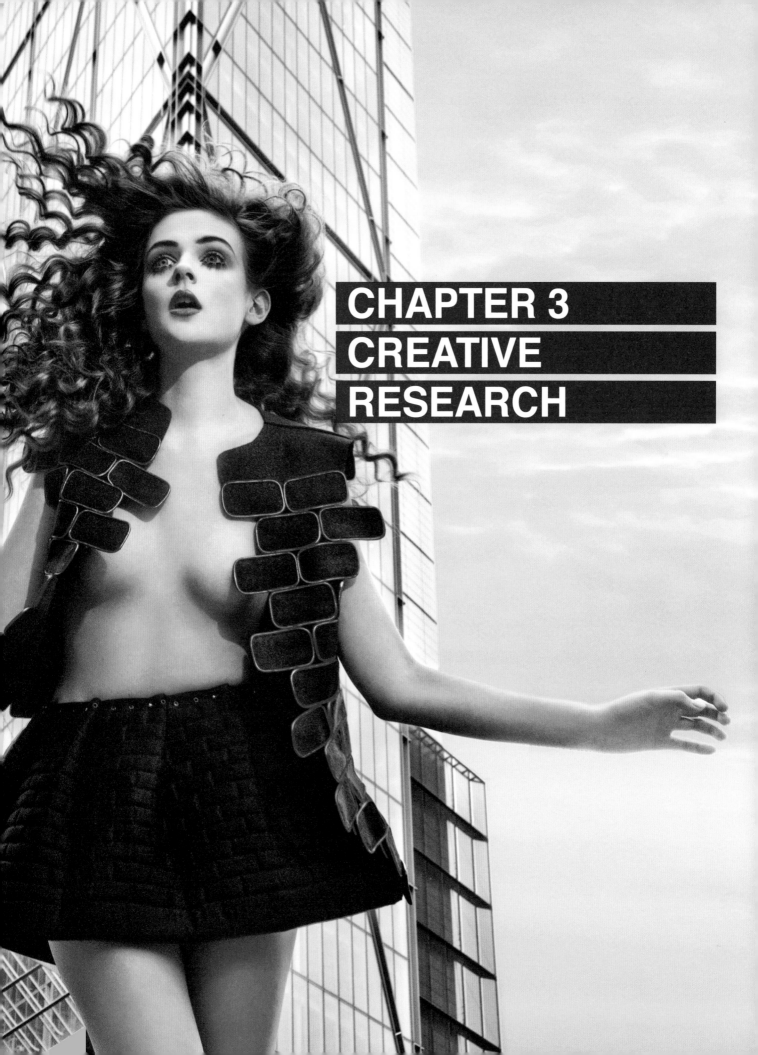

CHAPTER 3
CREATIVE
RESEARCH

Creative research is a milestone in the design of your final collection; it kick-starts the creative process of its design. Previously you researched and analysed markets and trends. Keeping in mind the information collected, you must now generate ideas and design and create the garments of your collection. These two stages, the first analytical, the second creative, require different mindsets.

When asked how he would describe the creative process, the French sculptor Rodin answered: 'First I experience an intense feeling, which gradually becomes more concrete and urges me to give it plastic shape. Then I proceed to plan and design. At last when it comes to execution, I once more abandon myself to feeling, which may prompt me to modify the plan.' (Cited by Johannes Itten in the *Theory of Color Design*, 1961.) Creative ideas often find their origin in, and are inspired by, experiences or influences that resonate strongly with the designer or artist; it is the 'intense feeling' Rodin mentions. Creative research looks for such inspiration in the hope that it will feed the designer's creativity throughout the design process.

For her collection 'The Dream Life of a Family of Monsters', Camille Bellot found inspiration in human and animal parts bound to provoke emotions. (See case study on page 164)

FINDING INSPIRATION

Inspiration is the spark that fires creativity. While creativity is sometimes understood as producing something from nothing, more generally it is seen as the transmutation or transformation of something already in existence. This starting point is the influence or inspiration of a creation.

Fashion designers often name a woman as the earthly muse who inspires them. Catherine Deneuve, for example, was Yves Saint Laurent's appointed muse over several decades. The muse, however, should not be confused with the woman who represents the target market of the collection as described in Chapter 1. Today's fashion muses are often famous women whose endorsement of a collection is also useful for communication and marketing.

Creative research is an alternative and reliable source of inspiration. While the next chapter, Development and Sampling, is focused on producing new ideas for design, creative research is an exploration during which you will consider and analyse material produced by others. It is very much a personal journey in search of material that will inspire you.

This material need not be related to fashion or garments. It can take the form of an image, idea, emotion, experience or narrative. As you approach this material, you must observe the effect it has on you. Does it interest you and why? How does it stimulate your creativity? Like Galliano you may be fascinated by ethnic and historical garments, or like Roberto Cavalli you may find the animal kingdom an endless source of design and prints.

You may decide at one point to investigate further certain aspects of a subject. If you were to choose the early twentieth century Art Deco movement, for example, you would need to get a better knowledge of the styles and achievement of that period. Through your research you may notice that the streamlines which first appeared on the automobiles of that era found their way into many other areas of design. Streamlines had enormous cultural significance and are powerfully evocative of the 1930s. By getting a full understanding of the dynamics and mechanics of your subject, by becoming an expert on your chosen theme, you increase your ability to use and transform it. You should also seek to make this research subject you own, to appropriate it and seek an individual and subjective perspective. Both expertise and individual point of view should be visible in your research files.

Eventually you will narrow down the influence of your collection and, in order for it to effectively inspire your creativity during development and sampling, you will gather a selection of material, visual or text, onto a theme board. This theme board is destined to be the 'design gene pool' of your collection while the remainder of the material gathered will not only contribute to your understanding but constitute a reserve of inspiration.

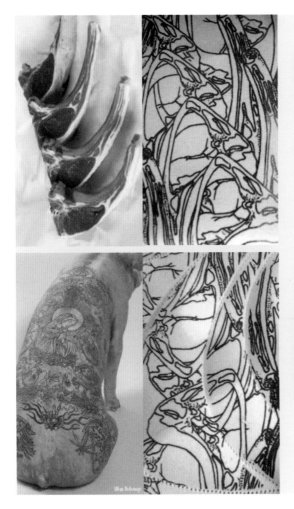

...that fashion (...) stinks»

Leigh bowery

Convergent And Divergent Thinking

Convergent thinking is what you do when you try
to solve a mathematical problem. It requires
focus and attention. It has a starting point
and a conclusion and ideas in between are
logically articulated and progress step by step,
converging towards the one correct solution.
When you analyse a subject such as your market,
you rely mainly on convergent thinking.

Divergent thinking is used to generate ideas
and creativity. It does not attempt to find
the one correct answer but to produce as many
valid propositions as possible. This mindset
is typically used in brainstorming. Divergent
thinking favours association of ideas and relies
on perception rather than logic. It is playful
and does not require concentration but rather an
awareness that welcomes influences and new ideas.
It benefits from a meandering approach and rarely
has one single starting point or conclusion.
Divergent thinking allows one idea to lead to
another and to be pushed further.

While you will be relying mainly on divergent
thinking during the creative process, from time
to time you will need to review and select from
among all the ideas you have generated, those
that best answer your brief. This selection will
demand that you exercise critical judgement and
will rely on convergent thinking.

To produce a successful collection, therefore,
you will need to balance the convergent and
divergent thinking that support critical
judgement and creativity in light of the
understanding you have acquired of your market
and competition.

While coming up with truly original design is
not easy, students often fail not because of a
lack of creativity but because they are unable
to edit or discard many of the ideas they have
generated. Often students maintain a false sense
of security by packing their designs with too
many features.

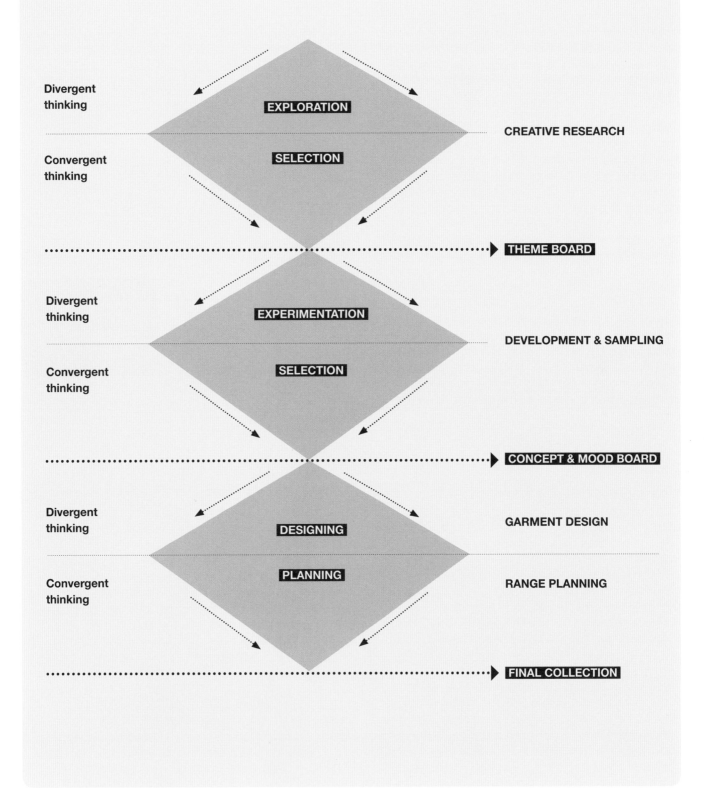

Divergent
thinking

EXPLORATION

CREATIVE RESEARCH

Convergent
thinking

SELECTION

THEME BOARD

Divergent
thinking

EXPERIMENTATION

DEVELOPMENT & SAMPLING

Convergent
thinking

SELECTION

CONCEPT & MOOD BOARD

Divergent
thinking

DESIGNING

GARMENT DESIGN

Convergent
thinking

PLANNING

RANGE PLANNING

FINAL COLLECTION

YOUR SKETCHBOOK

A good source of inspiration is first of all one that affects you; it must be appealing and meaningful to you and is likely to be related to a personal experience. Such an experience may take place at any time and as a designer you must make yourself available to it, be willing to absorb it and ready to document it for later use.

Such records are usually collected in a sketchbook. Since this needs to be kept simple and accessible, a small artist's drawing book and a pencil usually work best, as you can easily take notes, draw, or attach other material into it. To complement this sketchbook you can also store and organize on your computer digital material you find on the web.

Your sketchbook is a good place to refer back to and look for ideas and inspiration; it is where your creative research should start. Think of your sketchbook as the unwavering witness of your creative life. If you have not yet acquired the habit of keeping one, now is a good time to start. You can instantly produce material for it by revisiting memories. Remember an experience that made an impression on you, consider the context in which it took place and the sensations that it evokes. Try to relive this moment and identify what makes it valuable to you. Finally, document it; you may want to look for images or you may choose to draw a picture or write a short text. All these things have a place in your sketchbook.

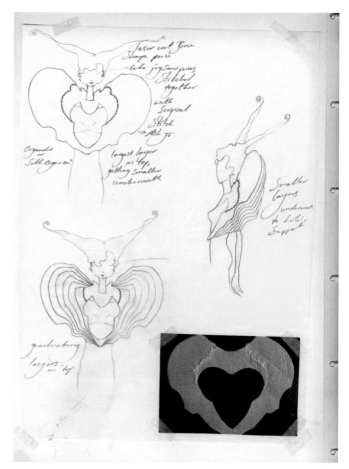

In her sketchbook Claire Tremlett's ideas quickly transform into garments. (See case study on page 170)

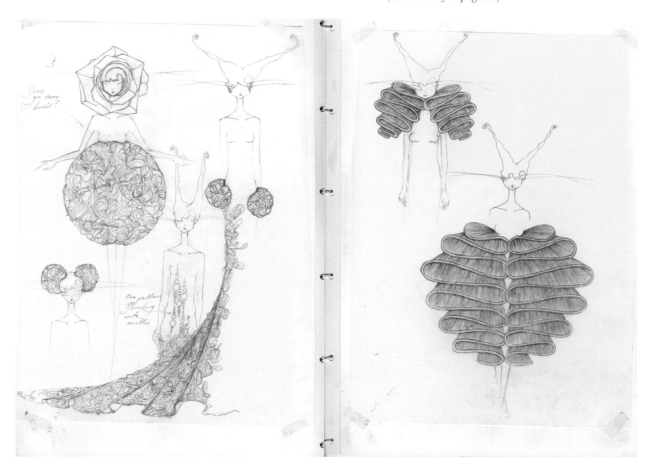

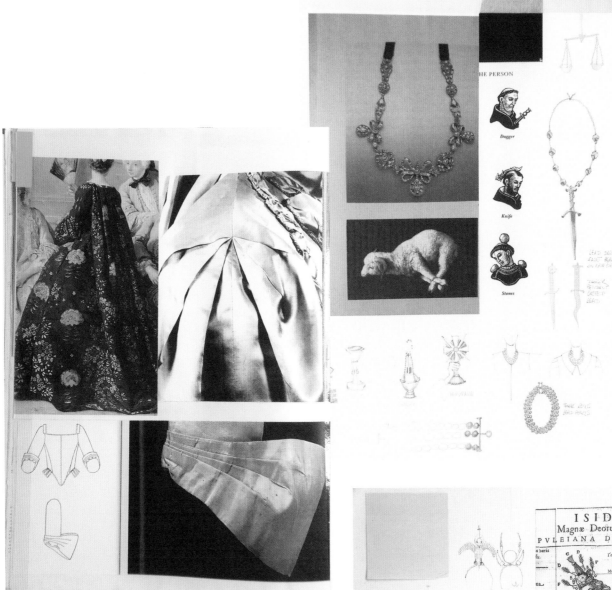

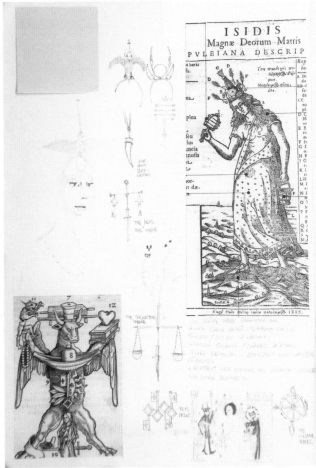

These extracts from Matthieu Thouvenot's sketchbook show how he has explored different aspects of his theme. (See case study on page 146)

POTENTIAL SOURCES OF INSPIRATION AND INFLUENCE

If your sketchbook does not provide a starting point for creative research there are specific subjects you can explore for inspiration, each with their own sources for information and material. There are no right or wrong sources of inspiration and influence; the list is endless. The following paragraphs intend to provide just a starting point.

As mentioned in Chapter 2, trend forecasters have identified different influences that affect the development of fashion. They include: societal and technological developments; youth culture and street fashion; achievements in the arts from architecture to graphics, film and music; celebrities and public figures; and of course current fashion. Any subject able to affect fashion trends may provide you with the ideal influence. Only the most recent manifestations of these influences are useful when identifying emerging trends; however their historical development may also prove inspiring.

These potential sources of inspiration are all 'man-made', that is *cultural*. Other cultural sources, such as folk or ethnic costumes and cultures, myths and legends, stories and narratives are of little value to trend forecasters because they are mainly historical, but they can be utilized by the fashion designer. Finally, the natural world and everyday life have provided inspiration for artists since the Renaissance.

Such themes can influence designers in one or two different ways. Some, such as the film *Death in Venice*, for example, are more likely to provide an atmosphere, an impression or a story. Others, such as the Art Deco movement, might be more concrete – their aesthetic and designs may be deconstructed and directly exploited. While they have cultural significance and evocative power, the design elements of some influences are so well defined that the two dimensions can be treated separately. Ethnic costume or a military influence, for example, can provide an atmosphere but also specific designs. Junya Watanabe's Autumn/Winter 2010–11 collection, for example, uses military detailing but the silhouettes and the atmosphere to which he refers are Edwardian.

Commercial designers often draw inspiration from the fashion industry itself, whether from past or recent work of other designers or trend forecast reports. High street fashion designers, for example, design according to formal trend forecasts, whilst designers in long-established fashion houses rely on the house archives for inspiration. Fashion labels must maintain a design identity and the designers' brief is often to *actualize* the house style, adapting it to be sympathetic with current trends.

Fashion students who choose their inspiration in the fashion world, must produce something genuinely new in order to avoid being accused of plagiarism. The student ownership of the final design must be obvious and its influence only evoked. This is in fact a very difficult exercise; one solution to this problem is simply to draw inspiration from a subject removed from fashion.

Influenced by manga and other comic strip drawings, Andrea Tramontan created these visuals that inspired his collection. (See case study on CD)

Inspiration for fashion design can be found in a wide range of current or historical subjects covering cultural, natural and everyday life.

'Clothing will eventually surpass housing altogether and function as the city dwellers final home'
– Kosuke Tsumara cited in Quinn, 2003

FINDING MATERIAL

While books, magazines and museums remain very good sources of information and material on most subjects, the advent of the internet has removed many restrictions imposed by physical location.

Relying too much on the internet for creative research, however, presents some drawbacks. Search engines favour popular websites and ignore material off the beaten track. The format of the internet weakens the experience it provides. The quality of visual material available is usually low resolution and there is a risk that the large quantity of material accessible reduces its impact. Time spent looking at images on paper or on screen rarely carries the same weight as first-hand experience, where details, movement, texture, size and proportion may make a strong impression on you. A picture of a fairground will never replace the experience of actually being at one.

Inspirational material can also be collected in everyday life, from the street, department stores, second-hand shops, flea markets or from nature. Travel can also provide useful material – as an outsider's perspective can be surprisingly stimulating.

An image only offers a certain point of view while first-hand experience allows a range of sensations.

MANIPULATING MATERIAL

The purpose of creative research is to find material that will feed your creativity. As you explore themes and subjects, new material might overtake that which was previously in your mind. Keeping hard evidence and documenting your journey in research files is, therefore, very useful. Looking back on the accumulated material, you will be able to confirm that you are making progress, or you may decide to explore a direction you have so far ignored.

Playing with this material will also help you to get involved with it and to strengthen your experience of it. Stimulating your senses and strengthening your perception of the material will foster divergent thinking and nurture your creativity. Depending on the nature of the material you have collected you can do this in different ways. You could simply sketch it or produce new visual or narrative material around it. You could invent an experience, the reverse of what you did when you explored your memories to find inspiration. You may have noticed an eighteenth-century dress in a museum, for example. While you look at it try also to experience it in other ways: imagine how it may move, what it must feel like to wear or what would happen if you were to unpick it and take it apart.

Besides sketching, you can produce visual material through collages or other visual manipulations by hand or digitally. The purpose here is not to transform the material to produce new designs but to gain familiarity with it and to forge a point of view in order to facilitate further exploration. Deconstruction, the teasing apart and analysis of the design elements of a style is also a useful way to manipulate the material you have collected. An influence is more potent if you have developed a close understanding of what makes it work and allowed for your own expression of an individual perspective on it.

If you have explored a number of subjects, you must eventually narrow down the scope of your interest. You may have found that in fact only a portion of the original theme actually inspires you. Once you have redefined the perimeters of your influences you should consider what remains of your original themes. Understand what attracts you to each one. Try to see if any are complementary. Perhaps lay down all the material you have selected for each theme and identify which you would like to retain.

Through digital manipulation of material, students can acquire a better understanding and familiarity with the result of their research, as illustrated here by Verena Zeller's work on a classic portrait. (See case study on page 158)

Valentine Cloix's mountainous landscape has been manipulated digitally. (See case study on CD)

CHOOSING YOUR INFLUENCES AND PUTTING TOGETHER YOUR THEME BOARD

Most designers work with one or two influences. Of course their number depends on how they choose to define them – if they do so in a very narrow way, they may consider more.

While naming your influence helps to set its perimeters, the material that you include on your theme board goes a long way in explaining how it might influence you, and showing which element of its design inspires you. If you select sea shells, for example, select pictures of shells you like for your theme board and highlight what makes them special, whether their shape, colour, structure or texture. The theme board will maintain your awareness of this material during the next stage of the creative process – development and sampling – when you will let your mind wander again to produce design ideas. What matters is not the quantity of the material gathered on the board but its inspirational qualities. A balanced theme board will include allusion to an atmosphere, direction for aesthetics and elements of design. It is preferable to include as few fashion references as possible, as the influence of the garments depicted may become overwhelming. Store the remainder of the material gathered during creative research in your sketchbook or research files so that it is accessible for future reference.

Dez Bara's theme board for his S/S 2011 collection is evocative, personal and poignant. (See case study on CD)

Inside Warts Out

Dez Bara Spring/Summer 2011

Wrapping Up

As a fashion designer you will constantly be on the look-out for inspiration. It is an exhilarating prospect that implies that you are open to the world and in turn willing to contribute through your designs.

Creative research has led you to gather and select the material shown on your theme board. This material must enthuse and excite you as it needs to sustain you during the next stage: development and sampling. This stage, both creative and experimental, also benefits from divergent thinking. To allow the material on your theme board to influence and inspire you, display it in a prominent place in your studio alongside your client board. Maintain a strong awareness of the material you have chosen to include on it – it will provide the 'design DNA' for your own collection.

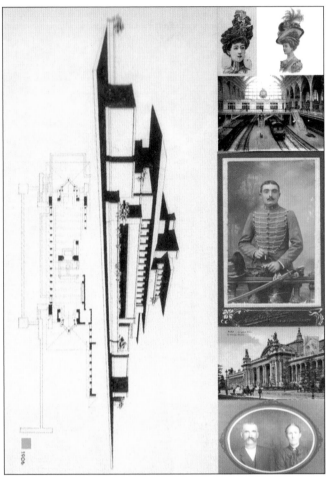

The layout favoured by Guillaume Dollinger and Alexandre Fléveau for their theme board is precise and controlled, reflecting the style of the garments they intend to create. (See case study on CD)

CHAPTER 4
DEVELOPMENT
AND SAMPLING

To answer the demands of their brief, fashion designers must take into account a number of parameters, ranging from marketing to technical issues. Creating a fashion collection is like putting together a jigsaw puzzle, each piece fitting with the next and together forming a picture.

Development and sampling (D&S) is a key part of the creative process, during which the material you gathered as a result of your creative research will inspire design ideas for your collection. Your primary aim is not to design full garments but to investigate ideas that may contribute to their design later. These design ideas may be seen as further pieces of the jigsaw puzzle; they must work together and contribute to answer the brief.

This chapter highlights activities that may help stimulate your creativity during D&S; it also recounts different techniques used in the design of garments. Its purpose is not to detail techniques you should be familiar with, but to recall them so you can consider all the options available to you.

During D&S you need to find a balance between playful exploration and your purpose. At some point during this process, the *concept* of your collection will emerge: the idea that explains your collection and makes it cohesive.

During development and sampling, Katya Babenko (OSFD) has used 3D modelling, observed and analysed through photography, to design patterns that will help her construct her garments.

YOUR STRATEGY FOR DEVELOPMENT AND SAMPLING

D&S is an experimental time. Seeking inspiration from the material on your theme board, you may use pen and paper to generate design ideas but should also spend time in the workshop making and trying things out. D&S is as much about creating as it is about designing. The realistic representation of your ideas through illustrations and prototypes will help you not only to evaluate and improve them but also to resolve any technical difficulties.

The construction of a garment is one of its most defining elements. The material used, however, must have qualities appropriate to its structure, and the fabric's texture, colours, finish and embellishments can significantly affect the overall design. Any element of garment design may be investigated during D&S but you must account for the fact that most of them are interrelated. D&S is also the appropriate time to source the necessary material and, if allowed, additional labour for production.

The process that follows D&S is normally dedicated to fine-tuning your designs and creating garments and it should avoid the introduction of new and complicated design ideas. D&S is, therefore, the time to be adventurous and ambitious; investigate as many design ideas as possible, balancing techniques that are familiar to you with those you wish to learn. In particular consider the different elements of design that you would like to develop and organize them logically in relation to the way they may interrelate. Identify all the resources available to you as well as any practical constraints; there is no point considering a design if it cannot be produced due to lack of skill, equipment, time or finance.

If, for example, you wish to work with leather, it is advisable to ensure access to the necessary equipment and source material before proceeding; they may prove expensive or not be easily available. If you keep in mind the practical restrictions that apply to you, you will not feel you have wasted time working on ideas that you eventually discard. In fact quite the opposite; this process will help you to focus on the most appropriate ideas and those you reject for this collection may be banked in your sketchbook for later use.

Setting a deadline to complete D&S will help you preserve time to effectively design and finalize the garments of your collection later. Allocate time according to the priorities of your institution (where most marks will be awarded), whether it is creativity of design, quality of make or presentation. Be decisive and move forward if you feel you have investigated all the ideas you need to design your collection.

At times, even the best laid plans can develop a life of their own. Be open to the unexpected; with the right attitude even accidental and fortuitous developments can lead to interesting results. Step back regularly, assess how your strategy is unfolding and revise it if necessary. If you feel you are stalling, change your point of view or adopt a different approach. You should welcome an external perspective and discuss your work with tutors and friends, too.

ELEMENTS OF GARMENT DESIGN AND CONSTRUCTION TECHNIQUES

Fashion designers cannot limit their work to pen and paper; their designs need to be feasible as garments that can be worn. To achieve wearable clothes designers often rely on tried and tested techniques. A designer's technical knowledge defines to an extent what they can design. The textile industry, for example, has developed **intelligent fabrics**. Without knowledge of what these fabrics can do and how they work, fashion designers cannot use them effectively. Similarly, fashion design students need good technical skills in order to produce their final collection, especially as they usually have to make the garments themselves.

Knowledge of materials and production techniques widens the type of designs that may be considered and helps estimate production costs, both in terms of time and money. However, fashion students may, like fashion designers do, also question the way traditional techniques are used and apply their creativity to adapt and even invent techniques.

Each of the following techniques and elements of design contribute to garment design. They are not listed in any specific order but they may affect each other and be interrelated. At this point you need not address the complete design of a garment but simply investigate some of its aspects.

COLOUR

Colours are not generic. Referring to 'pink', for example, is not specific enough and designers rely on a **colour model** to identify exactly which shade they mean. Perception of colour is a complex phenomenon that may vary with individual and context. Colours also have symbolic and cultural significance that affect how we perceive them individually and as a group. Colour trends cause certain shades to be popular at a particular time, in a given market. Beyond fast-evolving trends, some colours are more acceptable than others to some markets; while shell pink is regarded as sophisticated, candy pink is traditionally a younger colour.

To make successful use of colour in fashion you must be mindful of your own personal preferences and always consider your client's taste. Designers sometimes establish their colour palette – the range of colours with which they will work – from a picture or other elements of their theme board. Trends in colour are, however, far too important to ignore and colour forecasts are a good starting point; using forecasted colours also increases the likelihood that material and trims will be available in the colours you have chosen. Traditional fabrics, however, such as Chinese woven silks, are often available only in a limited range of colours. Finally, be aware that your costs are likely to increase with the number of colours you use.

Your palette should achieve harmony and evoke an image that is sympathetic to the theme of your collection and your market. Defining a palette, however, is not enough; perception of one colour depends on those surrounding it. You must, therefore, consider how you will use your palette: identify the block colours, the highlights, and how colours may be combined and in which patterns. Colour is a powerful tool and can complement other aspects of garment design. The balance of an asymmetric garment for example, may be adjusted with colours of different value or lightness.

Limit your use of colour or rely on neutral or traditional ones if you are not very confident in your dealing with it. By exploiting texture, designers such as Ann Demeulemeester, a member of the Antwerp Six, can produce exciting collections in a narrow colour range. Chapter 2 highlighted the seasonal use of colour. Traditional use of colour may also be affected by the garment's function, as demonstrated by activewear.

Mariel Manuel demonstrates an individual use of colour. (See case study on CD)

Clements Ribeiro, like Prabal
Gurung and Custo Barcelona, are
very confident in their use of colour.
These garments from their
S/S 2011 collections demonstrate
how print, contrast and line can
be used to strengthen a silhouette.
Their choice of colour is also
consistent with the forecast on
page 40.

Although the colour palette of Matthieu Thouvenot's collection is quite broad, each of its outfits relies upon one or two shades of colour at a time. (See case study on page 146)

Matthieu Thouvenot's colour palette derived from baroque paintings is confirmed by a floral print.

MATERIAL

Fashion designers need to be familiar with the fabrics that are available – their qualities, their cost, and also their traditional use – in order to select those most suitable for their designs. The weight, the handle or drapability, the hand (feel to the touch), the sheerness or opacity and the lustre of a fabric affect not only the look and feel of the finished garment but also its construction and manufacture. Depending on the function of the garment, other properties such as cover (warmth), ease of care, air and water permeability, strength and abrasion resistance may also need to be taken into account. Activewear, for example, demands strong, abrasion-resistant, absorbent and air-permeable material. Traditional uses of fabric, easily determined by observing garments currently in the shops, may be associated with practical or cultural considerations. Outerwear and jacket linings are soft and lustrous to help them slide over an already clothed body; acetate, rayon and lining silk are popular choices. Day wear in many markets requires easy-care fabric, while more delicate materials, such as silk satin, are reserved for evening and occasion wear. Until recently lustrous fabrics were culturally unacceptable for day wear in many Western societies – a convention eroded in the mid-1990s by Matthew Williamsons' silk skirts and dresses, reminiscent of underwear silk slips which, when worn with a cashmere twinset or sweater, were as suited for day as for evening wear.

Teaching institutions expect students to demonstrate a knowledge and understanding of these traditional uses of fabric. Beyond functional considerations, though, it is also the role of fashion designers to experiment and invent new ways to use fabric. Many of the qualities of a fabric are determined by the nature of the fibre used but they also vary according to the way the fibre is processed. Typically fibres are spun into yarn which is then woven or knitted and finally treated for finish. Silk fibre, for example, can be used to produce organza, satin and crêpe, each presenting very different qualities. Fibres can also be fused to produce non-woven material such as felt.

Natural fibres derived from plants, like cotton and linen, are cellulosic; natural fibres produced by animals, such as wool and silk, are made of proteins. Man-made fibres are often known under their trademark (e.g. Spandex). They may also be cellulosic, like acetate and viscose rayon, or non-cellulosic, in which case they are often derived from oil, like acrylic and nylon. Fabrics produced from man-made non-cellulosic fibres have poor absorbency and are mildew resistant. Worn close to the skin they encourage bacterial development and may cause body odours; their qualities are put to better use in outerwear.

The attributes of a fabric also vary according to the type of yarn produced from these fibres. **Filament yarns** are made from long strands of fibre, usually silk or man-made, that require less spinning; in contrast **spun yarns** are produced by twisting together shorter fibres. Spun yarns make soft, warm and light fabrics while filament yarns have the regularity required for smooth and lustrous materials such as organza and satin. The length of man-made fibres can be specified for filament or spun yarns, such as nylon and spun-nylon. Crêpes are usually made from filament yarns with a higher number of **turns per inch (TPI)** than necessary. It is this highly spun yarn that becomes matt and springy and gives crêpe its qualities. Beside TPI, yarn is also characterized as **single spun yarn** or **ply yarn** (produced by twisting several threads together) and by its **yarn count**, a number inversely proportional to the weight of the fabric it produces. An 800-count cotton, for example, is twice a light as a 400-count cotton. This relationship, however, does not hold across fibres, each having a different scale. Speciality yarns (e.g. stretch, novelty, chenille or metallic yarns) are usually spun by blending different types of fibre together to produce fabrics with specific qualities.

Traditional weaving techniques include plain, ribbed plain, twill, satin, pile and leno weaves. In each case the **warp yarn** (running lengthwise down the fabric) and the **weft yarn** (running widthwise) interlace in a specific and distinctive pattern that affects the look and the quality of the fabric. The satin weave explains many qualities of the fabrics named after it. It has the minimum amount of interlacing necessary; each interlacing is widely distributed and contributes to a smooth surface with a high sheen. This quality is often compounded by the use of filament yarn. Satin also wrinkles less easily than other weaves. The two faces of satin fabric – one of which is comprised mainly of warp and the other mainly of weft threads – can have different colours or qualities, as with crêpe-back satin. The low interlacing also makes satin a good candidate for bias cutting; with its smoothness and high sheen it is ideal for lingerie and evening wear.

Inspired by a flag flapping across his building, Jeremy Laing's S/S 2011 collection effectively explores the habit and movement of different fabrics: leather, knit, satin, etc.

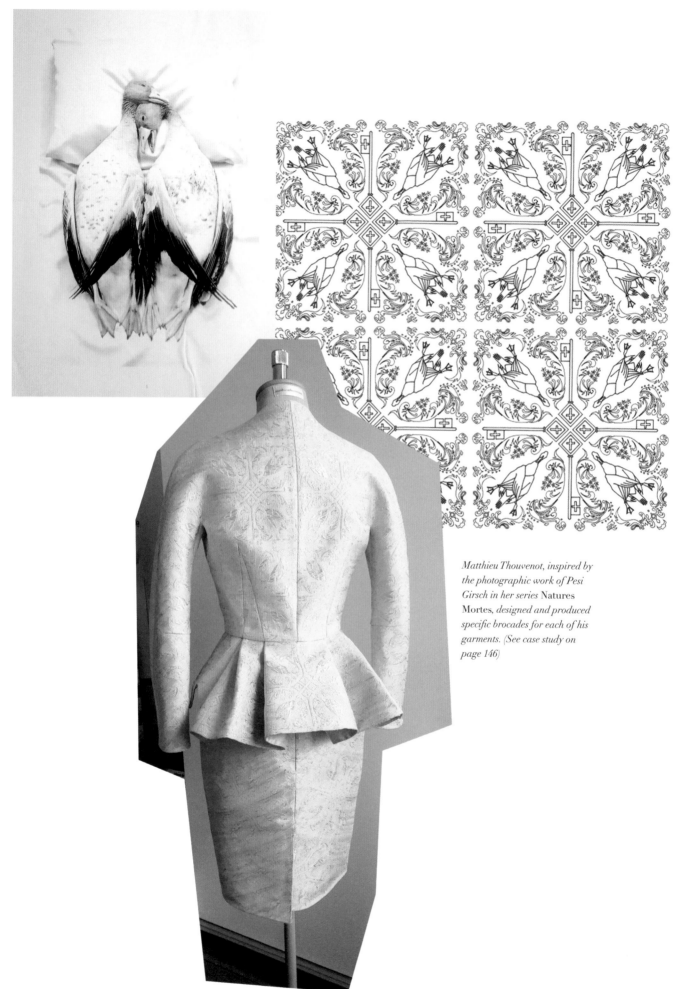

Matthieu Thouvenot, inspired by the photographic work of Pesi Girsch in her series Natures Mortes, *designed and produced specific brocades for each of his garments. (See case study on page 146)*

The pattern produced by the interlaced yarns of the woven fabric can also be exploited to produce fabric with either simple geometric patterns, such as dobby, or colour-and-weave (for example plaid), or more complex Jacquard patterns.

Fabrics may also be knitted. All knitted fabrics, whether produced by hand or machine, are different combinations of four basic stitches: knit, purl, miss or slip, and tuck. When the thread runs along the length of the knit it is a warp knit, such as tricot. When it runs across its width it is a weft knit, such as jersey and all hand-knits. Weft knits offer more stretch than warp knits. The comfort of any garment is increased by the ability of fabric to stretch but its design may be compromised if the fabric has no 'recovery power' – if it is not able to regain its original shape when stretched. Always test your fabric for stretch and elasticity. High-pile fabrics such as faux fur are usually knitted and, therefore, also offer some stretch.

Finishes with an effect lasting anywhere between permanent and temporary are usually applied at the end of the production process. Their purpose may be aesthetic (**calendering** and **mercerization**) or functional (coating, waterproofing and creating crease resistance).

Major fabric fairs, such as Première Vision, provide a useful opportunity to experience the vast range of fabrics available and discover new and innovative textiles. The lists of exhibitors found on their websites can be used to locate manufacturers and source fabrics. Fabric prices usually vary with the length purchased, and a minimum order length may apply. Never underestimate the length you require; there are noticeable differences in colour between dye baths, and discontinued stock may not be available for reordering. To identify a fabric exactly, the description provided by its traditional name must be completed by including the fibre used, the yarn count, the finish applied and obviously the width and length.

Students do not have to mass produce their collection and, therefore, are not restricted by continuity of supply. Recycled material – the lace from a wedding dress, for example, or the fabric from community workers' boiler suits – can be both cost effective and also contribute to the image and concept of a collection.

Despite the ever-expanding range of materials available, commercial designers often work with textile manufacturers to develop unique fabrics. You could consider a similar collaboration with a textile design student or a local manufacturer in order to increase the individuality of your collection.

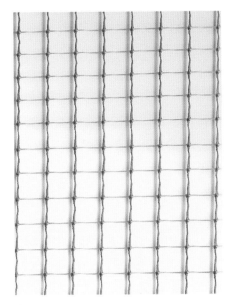

Cristina Sabaiduc produced her own materials using products from a builders' merchant: plastic mesh, caulk and rags. (See case study on page 134)

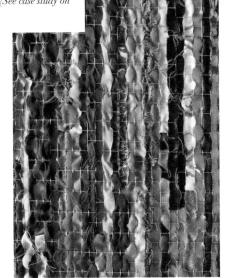

SEAMS AND GARMENT FINISHES

Seams are an important element of design; beside their practical purpose they can be used to highlight a detail or decorate a garment. They are used to great effect in commercial casualwear. The common seam, or running seam, needs to be overlocked or neatened if the garment is not lined. French seams, often needed for the fine and delicate fabrics used in lingerie, require two operations. Welt and flat-felled seams are strong but bulky and may be double topstitched.

The garment finish is an intrinsic part of garment construction; it has practical as well as aesthetic purposes. Some finishes, such as distressing techniques, are surface treatments but garment finishes also include hem finishes, topstitching, facing, ribbing, binding and lining. Garment finish can significantly affect customers' perception of quality and should be specified according to the market. A good finish requires time and skill. In the early 1990s the 'deconstruction' fashion trend promoted by Jean Colonna, Koji Tatsuno and Martin Margiela proposed garments that looked unfinished and were often constructed inside out. The reduced production cost of these garments also suited a time of economic slowdown.

Throughout his collection, Janosch Mallwitz has used a large variety of fabrics, each requiring specific finishes and machinery. (See case study on CD)

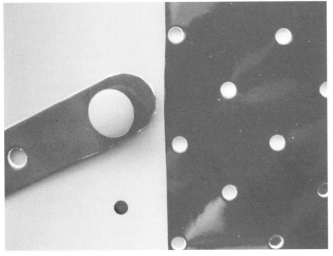

The modular nature of Cathy Amouroux's design required systematic perforation of the garment's material. (See case study on page 128)

These perforations, joined and tied by rivets, also from Cathy Amouroux's collection, allow material to be suppressed.

Sean Cabezas has layered fabrics of varying opacity and accentuated his style lines with bias binding.(See case study on page 176)

To finish the edge of her satin jacket Sophie Willett used single sides of zips, hijacking their functional purpose for visual effect. (See case study on CD)

SURFACE TREATMENTS

Surface treatments are either labour intensive or require specific technologies. They achieve different effects according to the stage of garment production and the extent of their application: they can, for example, be applied before cutting the cloth, on a specific part of the garment as a surface treatment, or on the overall finished garment. In addition to dyeing, printing, embellishments and fabric manipulation, surface treatments also include fabric finishes. While some modify the properties of fabric, most affect only its appearance.

Dyeing

Dyeing is a chemical process aimed at changing the colour of fabric. Yarn is often dyed before it is woven or knitted; in some circumstances fabric pieces and finished garments can also be dyed.

Dyeing alters fabric and may cause shrinkage. Different fibres take dye with different results, and the amount of fabric processed also affects the shade achieved. Dyeing fabric is a very effective technique; it is also an art. To avoid shading, it is recommended to dye fabric and garments in a single bath using professional dyeing equipment.

A number of special dye effects can be achieved either by **overdyeing** or resist dyeing. The latter technique can produce a variety of patterns by preventing the dye from reaching a certain part of the cloth, either by tying it (tie-dye, shibori) or by coating it with wax or resins (batik).

Printing

Printing is the application of dye on fabric in a pattern, either as a placement print or as a continuous repeat. Printing involves both a mechanical and a chemical process. Different results are achieved depending on the ink, fabric and printing technique used. Flocked, embossed and devoré fabrics are produced using traditional printing techniques in which the dye has been replaced by other chemical agents, respectively glue, Expandex and corrosive compounds.

The business of fabric printing is a difficult one. Industrial techniques are expensive to set up and require volume to be economically viable; on the other hand, fast-evolving fashion increases the risk of unsold stock. In response, a digital printing technology has been developed to be attractive for small runs; it is flexible and has no set-up cost. Printing your own fabric allows the use of different patterns within a narrow colour palette to strengthen the connection between the garments of a collection; students with access to traditional block- and screen-printing facilities or digital equipment should consider it.

Sean Cabezas's digital printing.
(See case study on page 176)

Sintija Reinfelde's shibori. (See case study on CD)

Fabric finishes

Long-lasting fabric finishes such as coating, stone washing, distressing (acid dye, enzyme wash, sand blasting and laser engraving) applied to finished garments produce very powerful design effects. White coating of finished garments, for example, has been a trademark of Maison Martin Margiela. Some of these finishes rely on complex chemical or mechanical processes and require industrial facilities. Crinkling and creasing is, however, easy to achieve through washing and the application of heat.

Embellishments

With a very few exceptions, embellishment techniques add decorations to fabrics through the use of thread and needle; they include embroidery, appliqué, cutwork, beading and the use of trims, zips and buttons, but also cords, braids, ribbons, rickrack, ruffles, lace, gimp and piping. Whilst in some cases machinery may be used, most embellishment techniques are labour intensive. Special needles and gluing techniques have been developed to increase production rates.

Fabric manipulations

Fabric manipulations are surface treatment techniques that use suppressions to achieve volume, draping, relief or texture. Fabric may be suppressed and held folded by pleating, smocking or tucking. It may be suppressed and held crushed by gathering or shirring. Reliefs can be achieved by cording, quilting and stuffing. Fullness can be added with ruffles, flounces and godets.

Fabric manipulations may have decorative purposes as appliqués but can also be used to create fit or volume in garment construction, thus contributing to the overall silhouette of the garment.

Perfectly synthesizing Italian and American styles of fashion, Alberta Ferretti garment designs use fabric manipulations, in particular twisting, tucking and draping, with effectiveness and economy. The same can be said of her use of embellishment techniques.

Tsolo Munkh relied on embroidery and cutwork to produce her vivid designs. (See case study on CD)

Valentine Cloix created 3-D fabrics through an unusual technique: vacuum forming or thermal moulding. (See case study on CD)

SILHOUETTE, FIT AND VOLUME

In fashion, **silhouettes** are very important; they are often what is best remembered and most commented upon in a collection. They can be discreet or dramatic; they can also convey a wide range of attributes from immodesty to authority. You should repeatedly consider the silhouettes of your collection, both during D&S and garment design. You may construct your garments to reproduce silhouettes you have drawn and selected, or silhouettes may emerge as a result of design and construction choices you have made.

The silhouette of an outfit is in part defined by the human body: the head, the trunk, the four limbs and their articulations; each part has a different shape and must have freedom of movement. Silhouettes can also be influenced by the season and the functionality of the garment; the silhouette of outerwear, for example, is likely to be less refined than that of an evening dress.

While garments must accommodate the human body, they also change its appearance and its perceived proportions. The construction of a garment, its silhouette and style/fit lines (the joining of different pieces of cloth cut in specific shapes to create fit and form) hide or underline parts of the body that may hold socio-cultural significance. Silhouettes can also be affected by accessories and styling; high heels, for example, elongate legs, while headgear increases the size of the head. Depending on the fabric used, the natural movement of the body may change the silhouette of the outfit.

The way the garment relates to the body also helps to project an image and identity. Balenciaga was famous for establishing a new relationship between a woman's body and the garment silhouette in the 1950s.

Construction techniques are similar to those of fabric manipulation: darts, suppressions, style/fit lines, smocking, gathering, pleating, tucking and shirring may all be used to achieve fit or volume to create different silhouettes. Volume may also be supported by quilting, stuffing, padding, stiffening, netting or boning.

Juliette Alleaume (Atelier Chardon Savard) created unusual and striking silhouettes based upon geometric shapes.

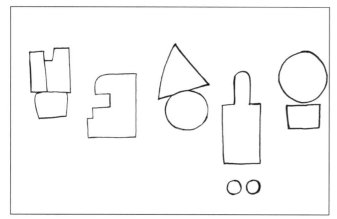

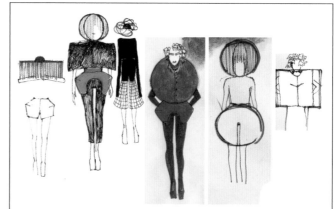

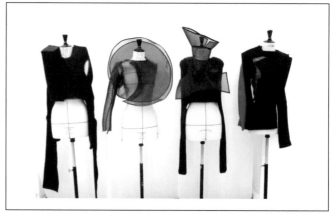

In the late 1950s Balenciaga came to the forefront offering new silhouettes. His outfits defined precise and simple volumes, not directly related to the woman's body but inhabited with obvious comfort. The work of his successor, Nicolas Ghesquière, has been celebrated for extending this spirit into the twenty-first century, as shown here in this A/W 2006 outfit.

DEVELOPMENT TECHNIQUES

The actual process of development is a personal one and techniques encompass two- and three-dimensional processes. D&S is about creating and making things; it is both a cerebral and a practical exercise. It progresses from creative research and starts naturally with work on paper or screen. Two-dimensional techniques are quick and easy to use. They include: drawing, colouring, painting, collage, photocopying and overdrawing. You can stimulate your creativity and generate ideas by manipulating and laying out such material in different ways to achieve juxtapositions, associations, contrasts or other transformations. The use of computer and digital techniques makes specific manipulations of 2-D material especially easy; they include filtering, negative contrasting, colour modification, distortion and overlaying. When experimenting with 3-D development techniques you may use cheaper materials than the one intended for the final piece; make sure, however, they have similar attributes and react the same way.

Your approach to development and your choice of techniques may affect your final designs, so an understanding of garment construction is crucial. You can try deconstructing existing garments to analyse their pattern, or re-engineering them by using some of their parts. You may also work on garment construction by using dolls as models, as Madeleine Vionnet did (the designer who introduced the bias cut in 1920s), or by building other forms of model (in modelling clay or other suitable materials), or by working from blocks, manipulating existing flat patterns or experimenting with creative pattern cutting through modelling and draping. Identify and adopt the approach that best suits your level of skills and your creativity.

Work on paper can be carried out in your sketchbook or, if you produce a lot of material, on loose paper sheets dated and stored in files or boxes for easy reorganization. You should also date and archive any 3-D material you produce, both for easy future reference and so that it is available for inclusion in the presentation of your collection. By documenting your ideas with photographs and drawings you may not only gain a different perspective on your work – 2-D and 3-D representations often highlight different problems – but also generate further material for your sketchbook and portfolio.

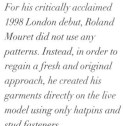

For his critically acclaimed 1998 London debut, Roland Mouret did not use any patterns. Instead, in order to regain a fresh and original approach, he created his garments directly on the live model using only hatpins and stud fasteners.

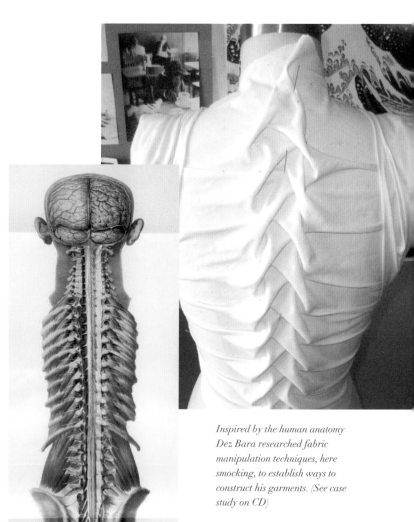

Inspired by the human anatomy Dez Bara researched fabric manipulation techniques, here smocking, to establish ways to construct his garments. (See case study on CD)

Generative Techniques

Techniques and processes are said to have *generative* qualities when they generate a design to which random or autonomous factors contribute. The random force of the wind, for example, is behind the music produced by a wind chime. Such generative systems disturb the relationship between designers and their work, since designers must relinquish some control of the output and focus their attention on the generative process itself. In the case of the wind chime, the only control the designer has on the music played is in the selection of the tubes and their associated notes. These generative techniques are especially interesting in that, once established, they usually require little attention from the designer and can be used repeatedly to produce unique but similar designs each time. Sometimes the process itself adds a new dimension and meaning to a design. Hussein Chalayan, for example, mixed part of his 1993 degree collection 'The Tangent Flows' with iron filings and buried it in his back garden, allowing the oxidation process to mark his garments and contribute to their design.

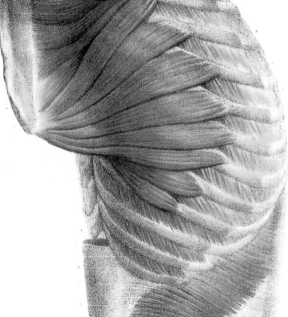

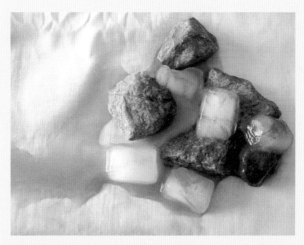

The technique developed by Tina Aileen of letting prepared cubes of frozen dye melt on her fabrics to produce a print is generative. Tina can select the colours mixed but the pattern is produced without her control. (See case study on page 152)

CREATIVE PRACTICES

During D&S, you should seek to be as creative as possible and try to develop a degree of freedom from conventional designs and techniques. Three different practices may stimulate your creativity and help you to produce and improve design ideas: self-imposed constraints, variations and pushing ideas to their limits.

SELF-IMPOSED CONSTRAINTS

The identification of a concrete problem to solve, such as financial or technical restrictions, is often the starting point of a creative response. Designers are often seen as problem solvers. Creativity is sometimes inhibited by too much scope – endless possibilities can make it difficult to find a direction and maintain focus – so the development of your collection may benefit from additional and self-imposed constraints. These may affect any elements of design; you may choose to design a collection using only vintage garments – men's silk ties, for example.

Or they could concern the construction of your garment. The 132 5. project led by Issey Miyake, for example, designs three-dimensional garments by folding flat, recycled material into geometric shapes in a way evocative of origami; like Chinese paper lanterns, they have volume but also fold completely flat.

Self-imposed constraints should be chosen with great care as they may have unexpected consequences. They should stimulate your creativity, not limit it. Be flexible and ignore those self-imposed restrictions when necessary. As students you are likely to have to explain such practices at submission; designers, however, reveal them to their public only when beneficial to their image.

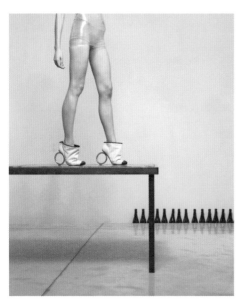

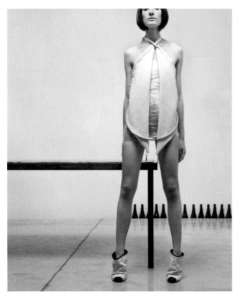

When she chose to design transformable accessories with two different functions, Irene Corazza (IUAV) added an extra constraint to her brief.

VARIATIONS

A creative idea may be investigated by producing and comparing as many applications and variations of this idea as possible. Variations can be produced by identifying the different parameters of your design and modifying them one after the other. You can change colour, material, proportions and so on. At times it may be effective to find a systematic way to produce these variations, one that does not require much reflection and may be automated. When designing a repetitive print, for example, you must choose both a motif and the way it is repeated. By modifying one of these two parameters you will systematically produce different prints.

This presentation by Yudai Seki (Musashino Art University) highlights how the slightest variations in cut can affect the silhouette. Designing a collection involves choices as to which elements of the design can be modified and as to when it is optimal.

PUSHING IDEAS TO THEIR LIMITS

Imagination and creativity are often inhibited by caution and habit. Good design, however, may emerge from pushing an idea to its limits. Being extreme will help to break down habitual levels of reserve, in itself a positive outcome even when the resulting designs are obviously excessive and impractical.

The purpose of this exercise is to help you discover new ideas or ways to implement them. It may also help you to better understand the *mechanics* of these ideas. This exercise may be carried out in at least two different directions; you may seek to broaden as much as possible the field of application of a design idea or you may focus on one single aspect and adjust its parameters, possibly to an extreme. The idea is to allow yourself the freedom to go as far as possible.

Upon completion of the explorative stage, review the work you have produced in a critical manner and try to learn from it. You may stumble upon new design ideas that may be exploited directly; other results may need to be toned down or stepped back to achieve a better design. This process may also help you to identify the essence of your design idea and gain a better understanding of what makes it work and how to best implement it.

Some designers, such as Viktor & Rolf, have made entertaining such extreme designs part of their trademark, as shown here in S/S 2011.

EXPLAINING HOW YOUR COLLECTION WILL WORK: CONCEPT AND MOOD BOARDS

Concept and mood boards are two complementary ways used by designers to express and explain their collections. While the chosen influence illustrated on the theme board exists independently of the designer and is used for inspiration, the concept of the collection is the idea that supports it and explains what makes it a unique proposition. The influence is exterior to the collection; the concept is at its core.

THE CONCEPT

A concept may contribute to the perceived coherence of the collection and its logic assists choices not only in garment design, but also styling and presentation. Vivienne Westwood, for example, has used many influences over 50 years of designing fashion, from bondage in 1976, to pirates and a number of other historical references in the 1980s and 1990s, but the unstated concept behind her collections has hardly changed. Her fashion, better described as anti-fashion, is fundamentally a political act; subversive and irrelevant, it seeks to question, through the use of bondage, corsets, crinolines or merciless footwear, the place of the female body in society.

The concept might be articulated as the way in which the designer interprets the chosen themes. A concept formulated as 'theme X meets theme Y', for example, highlights the designer's choice to bring two different themes together and how their interplay may explain the resulting collection. Junya Watanabe's collections often cross reference specific materials and prints with historical silhouettes and are achieved through his signature cutting technique.

Sometimes, when the designer has chosen one single influence, concept and theme share the same wording; in this case the collection represents the designer's interpretation of the theme. At other times the concept may take the form of a story, linking the individual designs into a collection, as with Hussein Chalayan's collections.

The concept of your collection may be clear to you early on and so can be used to guide you during D&S. Or one may emerge more gradually; as you move through the D&S process you will evaluate and select design ideas. Through this evaluation process a thread may become apparent that explains how your theme has influenced you and helped produce those design ideas. What do they achieve and express? The concise answer to this question could form your concept.

As you evaluate your ideas you should reject any idea that proves impractical because of technical difficulties or lack of resources. Retain only those that will be most valuable to the projected design. Not only should they be strong and have impact individually, but they must also be able to coexist within your collection. This selection will lead to the rejection of some ideas. It is very important, however, to be ruthless: good design requires coherence and a strong identity.

Concept of Janosch Mallwitz's Collection

The concept of my collection is graduation, an inevitable ending point and a new beginning. It is an intimidating and challenging time in which new opinions and beliefs are tried out and expressed with charming yet arrogant naivety.

Clothes may be used to conceal part of who we are and to try on a particular identity. I want to celebrate this fragile and stubborn mix of assertion and make-believe. Through technical romanticism – at once rough and luxurious – and through garments that dissolve into fragments, my collection represents the dynamics of individual reconstruction. (See case study on CD)

'I'm not like them, But I can pretend, The sun is gone, But I have a light, The day is done, But I'm having fun.' (Nirvana)

MOOD BOARDS

The concept of the collection is usually articulated in writing. In order to present it in a more descriptive way, however, it can also take the form of a concept board with images and added text. The evaluation process also goes a long way in helping you to put together your mood board – a selection not only of notes or drawings but also fabrics, colours and perhaps samples that illustrate the physical form your concept is likely to take in your collection. While the concept articulates the idea behind the collection, the mood board expresses its atmosphere and aesthetic. The former may be your compass, the latter your map.

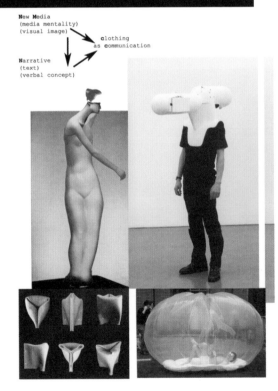

Mood boards explain how students intend to articulate their concept. Clockwise from the top, Andrea Tramontan demonstrates an atmosphere through graphics and colours, Mariel Manuel tells a narrative she has created, while Tatyana Kobikova is both explanative and illustrative.
(See case studies on CD)

Wrapping Up

D&S may be a playful exploration but it should result in producing concrete and effective contributions towards the design of your collection, pieces for your puzzle. Formulating your concept and establishing a mood board allow you to unify those different elements and express an idea of what your collection will be.

Another approach is to reorganize the work you have produced during development and sampling according to the three dimensions that define a garment: aesthetic, function and technique. This analytical perspective is not conducive to creativity but may prove useful if you feel yourself stalling.

With the next stage, garment design and range planning, you will define your collection as an association of individual garments. Eventually you will select a handful of outfits to demonstrate your style and express who you are as a designer. Beyond theme and concept, what matters is the impact garments have.

CHAPTER 5
GARMENT DESIGN
AND RANGE
PLANNING

The work you have done so far may have helped you to develop an idea of what your collection could look like. Guided by your concept, and using all the puzzle pieces you have gathered so far, from your target market to your mood board, you are now ready to give a definite shape to this vision.

You now need to plan your range, design your garments and produce them. **Range planning** identifies the types of garments your collection needs to include. If at this stage you have designed a series of well-defined silhouettes, garment design is mainly concerned with finding ways to construct and realize them; sometimes, however, garment design is an opportunity to build a collection around a few strong design ideas. Cut, Make and Trim (CMT), the effective production of your garments, is the last and most vital stage of the creation of a collection; it often sees stressed students struggling and competing for access to facilities.

As the deadline for submission approaches, it is more important than ever that you pay attention to practical constraints and carefully manage your resources. When project planning each of these remaining stages do not forget to account for the time it will take to complete the remainder of your course work too.

Commercial collections are able to spell out their style by presenting upwards of 25 outfits, along with variations on specific design ideas. Your collection must make a statement with all but a handful of garments, so every single piece plays a vital role. To make an impact and establish your style you must demonstrate a logic in the way you associate design elements into garments and combine them to create outfits or silhouettes. When accessible to the public, this logic helps to make an impact as people feel they have *understood* the design.

Verena Zeller researched and formulated the grammar of her collection through collage. (See case study on page 158)

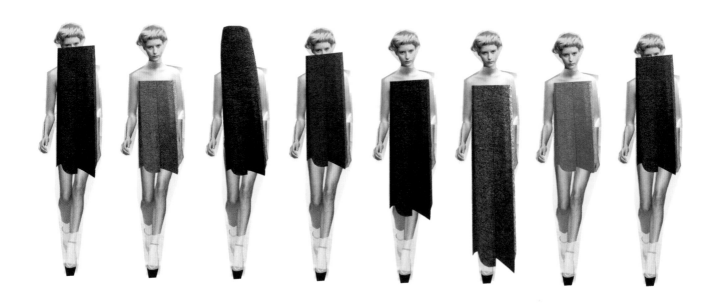

GOOD FASHION DESIGN

In most creative fields, rules on what constitutes good design are established time after time, only to be eventually rejected and rewritten. In the field of fashion it is the role of designers to contribute to this evolution, to find new ways to design beautiful garments. While they take into account trends and influences, fashion designers must synthesize them and give them coherence by formulating a personal style with its own logic and beauty.

GRAMMAR

In this context the word 'grammar' is sometimes used. Grammar commonly refers to the set of rules that helps to produce meaning through the association of words. With a limited vocabulary, grammar allows the production and understanding of an infinite number of sentences without the need to learn their meaning. By extension the notion of grammar is sometimes used in creative disciplines. Originally understood as the rules and principles of good design, it refers today to the *mechanics* of a given style; the formal or informal rules and principles followed by a designer. These may be formalized or may emerge from the design process but are usually self-imposed rules that specify how different elements of design relate and contribute to a coherent whole. It is this articulation between different elements, with its repetitions and variations, which contributes to a style and a **signature**.

Symmetry, for example, is one of the simplest and most effective rules of design; it is followed by the majority of garment designs and contributes to their harmony. When this principle is removed, special attention must be paid to the balance of the silhouette.

Outside the field of fashion, 'shape grammars' formulate sets of very formal rules for the production of shapes and patterns. These sets of rules are used by architects and industrial designers to produce innovative designs, identify improvements in existing ones, and deconstruct and analyse existing styles and products. In 1978, for example, George Stiny and William Mitchell wrote 'The Palladian Grammar', identifying 69 rules followed by the famous Venetian Renaissance architect, thereby enabling computer programs to design villas in the same style.

However, design grammars are rarely deconstructed and formalized to such an extent. Most are established through the repetition of associations and proportions and can be identified visually. As a designer you must train yourself to see and analyse designs this way, recognizing the internal coherence of a design and seeing how a grammar may constrain its variations.

In this work, Katya Babenko (OSFD) analyses the effect of symmetry on her garments. Symmetry/asymmetry is one of the primary rules of any design grammar.

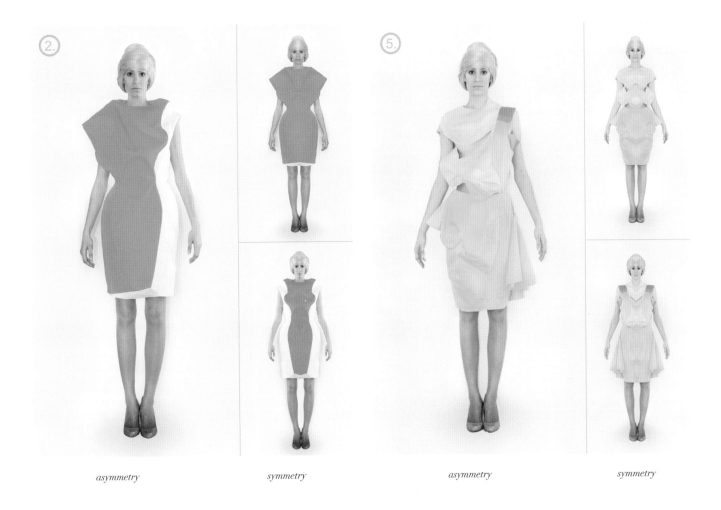

asymmetry   symmetry   asymmetry   symmetry

When you look at a fashion collection, identify both the common features and variations between garments. How do these illustrate the grammar of the collection? According to this grammar, modification of one element will lead to specific adjustments in others. When you review your own design, imagine the effect of modifying in turn different elements of its design. Your style and its logic may *forbid* some of these variations.

Your grammar may emerge naturally from this process or you may formally investigate and establish one, possibly through 2-D work. The latter will not only contribute to better designs but can also help you to generate ideas. While your concept explains how you have interpreted your influence, your grammar specifies how your designs work and achieve an aesthetic, the mechanics of your style. There must be a coherence between concept, aesthetic, grammar and style illustrated by individual garments and explained by your collection as a whole.

Hussein Chalayan's silhouette for S/S 2000 is short and extends away from the body in dramatic ways; the emphasis is not on texture but shape and colour.

Claude Montana's silhouette for S/S 1988 is fitted and long, with a nipped waist and underlined shoulders. There is texture and little colour.

GARMENTS: THE BUILDING BLOCKS OF A FASHION COLLECTION

Different types of garments traditionally combine into various outfits that fulfil practical and socio-cultural functions. Garments are either separates or full pieces. Separates are divided between top pieces (blouses, shirts, T-shirts, vests, waistcoats, jackets, knitwear and sweatshirts) and bottom pieces (skirts or trousers), each in different styles and cuts. A full piece is a garment sold as one that covers the whole body; this category includes suits, dresses, coats, catsuits and other all-in-ones. These garments can also be worn in layers and can function specifically as underwear or outerwear.

Each of these pieces of clothing has particular construction constraints and expected levels of finish, requiring specific design and production skills. In the industry, some labels and designers are known for their ability to design and make specific types of garment. In the UK, for example, Aquascutum is famous for coats, Karen Millen for dresses; worldwide, Armani and Chanel are known for suits. The types of garment you include in your final collection, and consequently in your portfolio, can affect the jobs for which you will be considered. Limiting yourself to just dresses, for example, will lead your grading jury and potential employers to question the breadth of your skills, so try to include as many different garment types as possible.

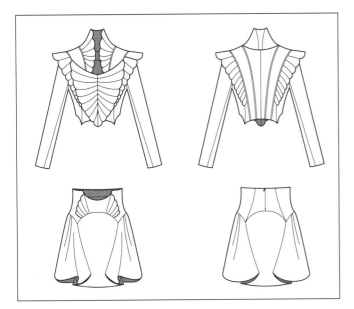

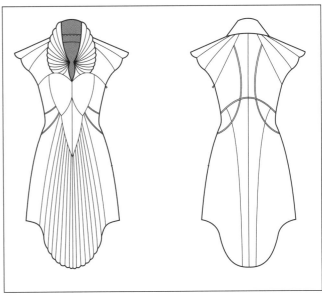

An ideal capsule collection will include a range of garments, separates and full pieces as illustrated by Bernice Chua's. (See case study on CD)

RANGE PLANNING IN THE INDUSTRY

Each fashion market requires a particular balance of different garment types. The numbers of top and bottom separates, for example, which can be sold on a market are linked. Designers and retail make choices based not only on aesthetic and style but also the types and functionality of the garments they include in their collection.

The process that leads to these choices is called range planning; it is a slightly different exercise for designers and buyers. Buyers select garments from amongst different collections not only with the aim that these garments sell but also in order to maximize revenues through cross-selling. Based on previous sales figures, sometimes analysed with the help of computer programs, retailers establish a range plan that specifies the types and quantity of garments they must order within specific price brackets. This range plan includes a balance of garment types (separates, full pieces, outerwear…) and a mix of sizes and traditional colours. It must ensure possible combinations into different outfits to be merchandized as *stories*.

With the same aim of optimizing revenues, fashion labels' sales teams and designers work together on a range plan. They take into account a wider range of factors, including the presentation of the collection and the mix of garments required to combine into complete and attractive outfits that demonstrate the designer's aesthetics. Some pieces may be included, despite low sales expectations, because they are central to the collection concept and necessary to its presentation. These are referred to as **window dressing**. They should have strong visual impact and be press worthy. On the other hand, fashion houses will also present buyers with garments that they have not felt necessary to show on the catwalk.

Buyers select garments from different collections and organize them into stories to propose to their clients. Designers organize their range around the concept and the aesthetics of their collection. They produce variations on each design within or across garment types, and select the most successful pieces to include in their collection.

Commercial designers often complete their range plans by offering fabrics and details variations of some of their designs, as shown here in this Valentino line-up from A/W 1988.

RANGE PLANNING A FINAL COLLECTION

Depending on the institution, students must submit a final collection of four to eight outfits for grading. The number of outfits, or **exits**, allowed on the catwalk at the degree show, however, may be different. Budget and audience attention limit the total number of outfits that can be shown, and this number must be divided fairly between the students. Despite its reduced size, your collection must present creative and commercially viable garments, establish an identity and a style, and demonstrate the variety of your skills.

Each piece must be selected with great care as it can significantly affect how your collection as a whole is perceived. You must not include pieces that have little demonstrative value, even to complete an outfit. Try to optimize each exit allocated to you. Some outfits may include outerwear, for example, that could be removed on the catwalk to reveal the rest of the outfit underneath.

In the industry, designing and range planning a collection are two clearly distinct activities; this boundary is often blurred where a final collection is concerned. Commercial designers benefit from the support of their workshop and can usually afford to produce garments that may eventually not be included in their collection. This flexible approach offers the possibility of fine-tuning. When designing your final collection you must manage your resources carefully. It can be a good idea, then, to plan the range of your collection early on.

Range planning a final collection requires identifying, organizing and coordinating silhouettes and garments. Depending on the confidence of your vision you can plan your collection in one of two different ways. You can work things through in 2-D, which has its limitations but is very economical. Visualize your collection coming down the catwalk. Draw the different outfits you see, evaluate them and identify any possible improvements. Make sure you are presenting a strong, coherent and balanced collection. Once you are happy with the result you can specify and draw the individual garments and allocate your time according to the difficulty of finalizing their design and production.

If you have not yet formed a vision of your collection, you may need to adopt a more piecemeal approach. Try to identify a starting point. Which design, investigated during D&S, best expresses your concept? What is the most ambitious garment design you have contemplated? Such a central design could become the mother piece of your collection. Investigate its design on paper; while you fine-tune it, record any variations you can think of. You can, for example, address and vary a silhouette by adjusting hemlines. Try to translate a design idea into different types of garment or play with colour and material. Consider how these designs fit with your concept and could contribute to the overall collection.

Eventually, a range plan will form a collection, often presented as a line-up as shown here with Lucy Zhang Shuai's. (See case study on CD)

Matthieu Thouvenot's line-up. (See case study on page 146)

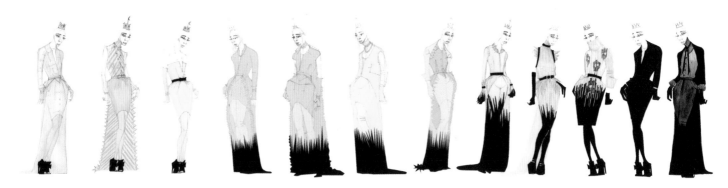

GARMENT DESIGN

Garment design is the penultimate step in the creation of your collection; the amount of work it will require depends on your progress during D&S. Most of your range planning and resulting garment design is likely, up until now, to have been on paper. You must now return to the workshop to cut your pattern, make your toile, test its fit, adjust it and finalize your design. It is one thing to draw garments but another to construct them effectively.

TOP-DOWN OR BOTTOM-UP?

Depending on the progress you have made on your silhouettes, your garment design will follow either a top-down or a bottom-up approach. If, during D&S, you have worked on silhouettes which were then completed and confirmed during range planning, you will follow the top-down approach. This involves figuring out how to construct those silhouettes by designing the corresponding garments, incorporating any other design ideas you have. The top-down approach is often followed in haute couture houses where the head designer expresses a vision by drawing outfits, leaving garment design to the workshop.

If you are not satisfied with the silhouettes you have produced, you will adopt the bottom-up approach. With this hands-on approach, silhouettes are, to an extent, the result of the combination of design ideas you use to construct your garments. You may, for example, have sourced a fabric you like and investigated a fabric manipulation you want to use; during garment design you will bring the two together to construct pieces of clothing within the constraints of the two choices you have made. In practice you are likely to mix both top-down and bottom-up approaches.

During garment design, you may have to give up on some of your design ideas because they prove impractical or too difficult to achieve. Also ensure that you have sourced all the material, trims and skills you need to complete the garments you have planned. Prioritize the design of garments that are significant for your collection or may be complex to design and produce.

Garment Development

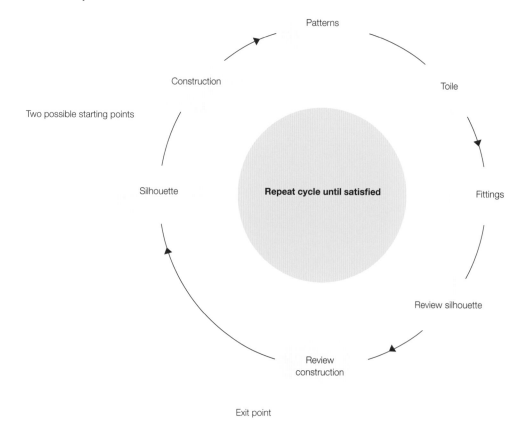

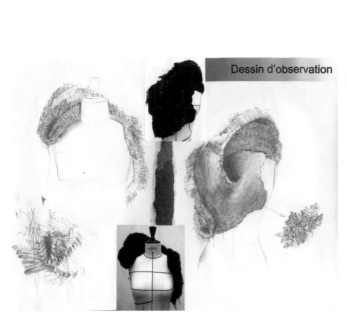

Dessin d'observation

*Tsolo Munkh reviewed her design
by observation and hand drawing
of her toiles. (See case study on CD)*

Dessin d'observation

PATTERNS AND TOILES

Once you have identified the best approach to garment design, you can select the most suitable technique to create and cut the patterns for your garments. You can flat pattern-cut from blocks or from existing patterns; alternatively you can model or drape your garments on a mannequin. Unless you are addressing a market that requires a specific sizing, make sure you work to the size chosen by your institution; it may have been chosen to fit catwalk models and differ greatly from commercial measurements.

Time spent on refining patterns usually helps reduce the amount of adjustments to toiles, or muslins; it may even cut down the number of toiles you will need to make. On this basis decide when you are satisfied to move from pattern cutting to toiling. Use an inexpensive fabric that is likely to react in a similar way to the cloth chosen for your finished garment; in particular it should be of identical weight and handle. Depending on your skills, the progress of your design and the quality of fit you want to achieve, you may need to produce multiple toiles for each garment. Note that depending on the production techniques, the 'prototype' piece may not be referred to as a toile; fully fashioned knit refers to swatches and samples instead.

Overall the process of garment design may be seen as a cycle; depending on your approach it may start either with silhouette or garment construction. Garment construction may be defined by the silhouette or by other design ideas. Patterns are cut to reflect this garment construction and a toile is produced on this basis. The toile is reviewed for construction, fit and design; this review may lead to adjustments to the silhouette and to the garment construction. Patterns are adjusted accordingly. A new toile

may be produced to be reviewed again and this cycle repeated. Sometimes the slightest alteration can make or break a design; do not stop until you are fully satisfied.

The toile is the closest representation of the finished garment you have; make good use of it to review design, construction and fit. Try as much as possible to consider the point of view of your market. Address how each garment sits within your concept. Does it do what you intended it to do and does it work with the rest of your collection?

To review your design you must be able to look and see. As mentioned in the previous chapter, 2-D representations give a different perspective on a 3-D design; some people also find that drawing helps them to analyse what they see. Take the time to look at your toile from different perspectives and consider the different elements that could be adjusted or modified in turn. Ask yourself what would happen if you modified proportions or changed details, style lines, fabric, or trims and embellishment. In particular review the silhouette. Is it balanced and in proportion? Should elements be added or removed? How do the style/fit lines flow and are they interrupted in the right place? How does the garment move?

Finally try the garment on a real person, not just a mannequin, as it is likely to react differently when worn and in motion. Check where the fit needs to be improved. Consider the overall construction of your garment, its foundation and finishing. Can you think of a better way to produce it?

*Marilou Dadat's toiles for her 'hang'
coat show the construction of shoulders
used in other pieces of her collection.
(See case study on page 140)*

CUT, MAKE AND TRIM (CMT)

Cut, Make and Trim, or CMT, the industry term for production of the final garment, is likely to be the most exciting and stressful moment in the creation of your collection. Most designers get a thrill when they see their garments in the final fabric; until this point it is, in fact, difficult to predict with certainty that a garment design will work.

CMT is vital to the realization of a collection and the time it requires should not be underestimated. The proximity of deadlines leaves little time to resolve any remaining problems. Compounding those issues, CMT is a bottleneck in most institutions, as students all try to access machinery and support at the same time.

Timing is vital, so consider CMT only when you are totally satisfied with your toiles and you have allocated your cloth between all the garments of your collection. Avoid cutting any fabric before this allocation, but ensure enough time remains to finish your garments to industry standards. Quality of finish will be graded at submission but is less vital for the show. A detail seemingly as benign as hanging threads will, however, be extremely visible on the catwalk and will let your collection down. Your institution may also require you to produce at least one of your outfits at an early date to include in promotional material.

You will face many more problems during CMT than you think. To reduce your stress levels be very well prepared and try to pay greater attention to details. Ask tutors, technicians and former students how to best negotiate this last hurdle; they will have experienced any specific problems you might encounter with the institution's facilities.

Most importantly, ensure that you have sourced all the material and trimmings you need. Imagine being unable to finish your garment simply because you have not found the correct zip.

The final fabric in which you will produce your garment is very likely to react differently than your toile, despite your efforts to match it. Test disposable cuts of this final fabric on all the machinery you will use, from sewing to buttonholes. In particular, pay attention to the gauge and sharpness of the needles and check the damage caused to the fabric by unpicking your stitches. If you are using several fabrics across the collection, it is advisable to make in turn at least one of the garments planned in each cloth to fully test your production capabilities.

Finishing usually takes more time than anticipated and requires specialist machinery – for buttonholes, for example. Make sure this equipment is available and take into account that it may have to be shared. With every use test all the settings of your equipment: thread, tension and needle according to cloth – they may have been changed since you last used the machine. Avoid having to unpick; it is damaging to the fabric and wastes time.

Make sure your work area is clean, and always protect and put away your garments when you have finished working with them. Pressing, the final finish, should be done with care as it can ruin your garment and leave you with no time to make it again.

Finally, if you are allowed and intend to use external help for CMT, make sure you communicate all the required information and material; this will include patterns, technical drawings and illustrations as well as cloth, trims and thread. Depending on your level of skills, outsourcing CMT can prove more work; all this information does not need to be formalized if you CMT yourself.

Cut, Make and Trim is a time when all the pieces of your design finally come together and all the dots are connected, as explained here with humour by John Galliano in A/W 2000.

Wrapping Up

Garment design and CMT must be approached practically and timed to ensure your collection is ready for the set deadline. Garments are evaluated as individual pieces both on the basis of their design and also the quality of their make and finish. As made evident throughout the last two chapters, the designer's technical skills and knowledge will directly affect these factors.

The work of a fashion designer, however, must extend beyond individual garment designs. Individual garments do not create fashion but collectively, as a succession in the form of a collection, they may demonstrate a style and an aesthetic. In time designers may establish a personal grammar – design 'rules' that define what constitutes good design in their eyes. The garments of such a designer can be recognized without recourse to the label inside.

Fashion, however, is mainly what happens when people wear garments. This notion must be ever present in designers' minds. They must not think of a garment as a finished, determined and steadfast product but as an entity that fully interacts with people and their lifestyle.

The successful presentation of the ISSEY MIYAKE A/W 2011 collection underlined the logic of its design, connecting it to a well-known style and explaining its evolution.

**CHAPTER 6
STYLING AND
PRESENTATION**

Like garment design, the way we combine and wear clothes constantly evolves. Sometimes youth groups, such as punks, hijack the traditional function of garments and use them to make a strong statement. Most of the time, however, this evolution is slow and with a longer-lasting impact; in the 1980s, for example, sportswear would not have been worn as casualwear in the way it is today. Only when women adopt and wear a style will it become a fashion. How women choose to combine and wear garments also affects fashion.

Like those affecting garment designs, these trends may 'bubble up' or 'trickle down' (see page 39). In addition to proposing new garments, fashion designers contribute to fashion by prescribing how to wear them. Presenting the garments in context also helps establish their relevance. The activity that pulls these presentations together is called **styling**.

At this point in time you have established your range plan, and designed and produced the garments of your collection. Now, in an academic environment, you need to present your collection on two different occasions: the end-of-year catwalk show and your submission to the jury. On both occasions you need to demonstrate how you intend your garments to be worn in a way that both helps explain their design and contributes to your achieving the best grade possible. Upon graduation you will then need to consider how to present your collection in your portfolio; this is addressed in Chapter 7.

PRESENTATION OF FASHION

Every season designers try to anticipate the fashion of the next, but when their garments reach retail they are unknown to the public. Fashion labels have a short window of opportunity in which to present their work and convince customers to buy it. These presentations often try to contextualize the garments; they can be shown worn by a model in a way that evokes a mood and demonstrates a context in which they might be worn. Labels use a number of tools, techniques and media to compete with other designers and communicate their vision to the public.

Trade salons and fashion shows play a vital role in this communication; they address wholesale buyers directly and, through media coverage, the clientele and the wider public. Store windows, retail merchandising and the stories put together by wholesale buyers all show how to coordinate and wear the latest collection. Communication in the media and on the internet – usually through still pictures and, increasingly, videos – is used not only to show garments but also to establish and maintain the image of the label and advertise its style. Each strand of such communication strategy must be effective and coherent in order to attract and hold the attention of a sophisticated, savvy public.

The simplicity required for pack shots still requires effective styling. This is well illustrated by Mariel Manuel's work. (See case study on CD)

Presentation of fashion on a catwalk is a tool used both in the commercial and the academic world. It requires strong styling. The collection presented here is by Andrea Tramontan. (See case study on CD)

PRESENTATION OF THE FINAL COLLECTION

When you present your final collection, whether on the catwalk or in front of a jury, the public you address is different than the one the industry seeks to attract. You are fulfilling an academic requirement and your purpose is to achieve a good grade, not sales. There are, however, similarities between fashion presentations in these two different environments.

In the commercial world, showing a collection on the catwalk is an expensive but vital part of a label's communication. A poor show may seriously damage the hard work of the previous six months. Students must present their collection on the catwalk, in conditions close to those in the industry, in order to be prepared for this professional requirement. The catwalk presentation usually contributes to the overall appraisal of the collection and may be independently graded.

Students also submit their final collection for grading, usually by a jury of several people. Garments are presented alongside supporting documentation of the student's work, from creative research to pattern cutting. Individual teaching institutions will specify exactly what is required, but your work is likely to be graded on the evidence that you have fulfilled the different 'learning outcomes' specified in the description of your course. These usually cover creativity, commercial viability, technical skills and communication. You must ascertain what the jury will be looking for to submit and present your work to your advantage.

Students may be required by their institution to present their collection in several ways, usually on the catwalk and in front of a jury as here for Verena Zeller's collection. (See case study on page 158)

FASHION STYLING

Styling expresses a style by coordinating garments and demonstrating how they can be worn. It also contributes to contextualizing the garments and establishing an image or identity, even if their design is relatively classic. This is achieved by evoking a context, an atmosphere or telling a story that adds weight to the style expressed.

Designers often rely on stylists, people specialized in garment styling, to express and bring their vision to reality. To that aim stylists usually coordinate garments with accessories, hair and make-up. A simple choice regarding footwear, for example, can not only denote the season and the time of day the outfit is intended for, but can also indicate the market targeted as demonstrated by the two presentations of the Jean-Paul Gaultier coat on pages 18 and 19.

Depending on context, the responsibilities of stylists may extend further and they may fulfil a role closer to that of Art Director. With the aim of orchestrating the audience experience, they may consider any elements that contribute to it. These may include quality of picture finish, location, set design, lighting, music, staging and choreography. Alexander McQueen, for example, was famous for the dramatic presentation of his collections. The styling and staging of his Autumn/Winter 1998–99 show relied on the influence that inspired the collection: Joan of Arc. When garments were not designed to envelop the head, models wore masks that evoked chain-mail and wimples (medieval headdresses). The soundtrack was overlaid with the sounds of a crackling fire and for the finale the stage was set ablaze (see page 32).

Styling may be creative, even outrageous, but should complement and not overwhelm the garments. Styling concepts are formulated either visually or as a narrative and are usually presented with the aid of story and mood boards. They may set out to shock

THE DIFFERENT CONTEXTS OF FASHION STYLING

	LIVE	PRINT	VIDEO
If the stylist is working with: A SINGLE COLLECTION OR FASHION LABEL	**Fashion show:** Paramount to the presentation of a collection to the market	**Look book:** Simple styling for pack shot pictures focused on presenting garments of a collection **House promotion:** Similar to promotion video but for printed material	**House promotion & other creative collaborations:** To present new collections but also to promote a brand across several lines such as accessories, fragrance and clothing
If the stylist is working with: MULTIPLE FASHION LABELS	**Personal styling:** Source garments and accessories, recommend hair and make-up to individuals, often celebrities	**Editorial:** Establish the 'story' told by photographs produced for and shown in fashion press **Print advertising:** Styling of clothing for models in adverts for products other than fashion	**Film advertising:** Similar to print advertising

or comfort. Visually they can play with light, movement, texture, colour or structure and express a level of warmth, femininity or androgyny, sensuality, glamour or rawness. They may also refer to a narrative that may be mythical, historical or cultural. More simply they often signify a market and a time of year; accessorizing a collection with sandals and sunglasses clearly identifies the season for which it is intended. The styling concept may be in sympathy or in contrast with the style of the garments. Very glamorous clothes can be shown effectively in a raw environment; an old factory or a meat market, for example.

When styling a collection for its promotion, garments and accessories are selected from within the fashion house itself. These garments should not only be shown to their best advantage but their presentation should also contribute to an image formulated by considering the concept of the collection, the garments to be styled and the people addressed. One single styling concept is usually used for the catwalk with identical styling repeated across the collection. The same concept is often used for other media and adjusted only within narrow limits. The image established in this way is easily recalled and can become a major marketing tool.

The same outfit by Tatyana Kobikova, shown in a location shot and in a photo-montage, reveals different qualities. (See case study on CD)

STYLING YOUR FINAL COLLECTION

Students must style their collections both for the end-of-year show on the catwalk, and to document their garments with **pack shots**, editorial pictures and, more rarely, videos to be included with their submission to the jury and also in their portfolio. Here styling may attempt to highlight the collection's concept and aesthetic. Such styling should be purposeful, controlled and individual; it should contribute to an exciting and memorable visual experience.

In fact, you already started styling your collection when you planned the range and organized your garments into outfits. Trying and styling these outfits is a good way to see if they work as expected and review their silhouettes. Kick-start styling well before you have finished CMT so you have time to revise your outfits if you feel they do not work as intended.

You will probably style your collection for the catwalk show yourself, but you can collaborate with a fashion communication student to style your pictures. Practical and financial constraints on styling will vary in both these situations. This does not mean that you cannot rely each time on the same styling concept or use the same props and accessories, but you need to appreciate which elements can be exploited to express your vision fully. You are competing for the spotlight and styling is a powerful tool that can make or break a collection; do not let limited resources prevent you from being ambitious and creative.

Like designers in the commercial world you may consider showing your garments on video. This may be achieved simply by filming your end-of-year show, or by producing a more creative video. The technical and creative complexity of such a project requires an elaborate concept and collaboration with a specialized team.

Valentine Cloix has manipulated this image to strengthen her presentation in line with the concept of her collection. Mirroring the images recalls a mirage, one of the themes that inspired her. (See case study on CD)

CATWALK STYLING

In the industry, catwalk styling may rely on accessories, hair and make-up, models, stage sets, props and music. However, in the academic environment you will be sharing the stage with other students, so it cannot be styled for your collection alone, and if you share models, they will have to have a generic style of hair and make-up. The elements you can usually control for your individual collection are shoes, headwear, scarves, glasses, props and other accessories; you should also select your music with great care. Depending on the number of outfits, however, providing accessories for all of them can prove expensive so you may have to manage your styling carefully and creatively.

Catwalk styling needs to be strong and dramatic, as each outfit is viewed for only a few minutes and from afar. The type of lighting used may affect your chosen colours in different ways; the distance and level of the stage in relation to the audience may render some details less visible. Rehearsals are very useful to make final adjustments and achieve the best impact. They are, however, often too expensive to organize and, in this case, you will have to try and visualize your looks coming down the catwalk to review their effect. On the day of the show backstage is mayhem and you may not be allowed access. In any case, organize and store the accessories for each outfit in a separate bag; include a detailed list and a picture showing how they are to be styled. If possible explain your styling to the dresser.

In the industry catwalk sets are designed specifically to contribute to the presentation. Sean Cabezas presented to his degree jury a design of a runway set that illustrated and explained the concept of his collection. (See case study on page 176)

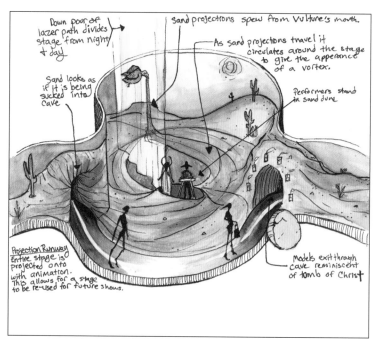

Sim Tan Au
Fashion Design
Women's Wear

5 of 6

Step 1: Wear the jumpsuit
Step 2: Let the model step into the dress first at the side. And then hang the collar part on her shoulder.
* Let the model hold the umbrella with one hand. And you assist her to wear.
Step 3: Close the collar strip with extra care. There is a buckle.
Step 4. Adjust the front pleat and back pleat. Adjust the direction of the umbrella. Semi open it.
Step 5. Remind the model to walk slowly and don't open the umbrella until she reach the runway downstairs.

Before the show Tina Aileen compiled illustrated diagrams explaining to the dresser how each of her outfits had to be worn and styled. (See case study on page 152)

EDITORIAL STYLING

Photo shoots are usually organized at your own initiative. They are a great way to show your garments worn in context and they will bring an extra dimension to your work. Inclusion in your portfolio will extend their use well beyond graduation.

Professional shoots can be very expensive. Photographers, models, and hair and make-up artists, however, are often happy to work free of charge and collaborate to produce 'test shots' – quality photographs they can include in their own portfolios. With a little effort you can easily put a team together. Contact fashion communication and fashion photography students; approach any friends or girls on campus who have the right look to model for you. Check the skills of each person in the team and identify responsibilities – in particular post-production (the retouching of digital pictures). Ask to see the hair and make-up artists' and photographer's portfolios. Before confirming your model, make sure she is photogenic and will look the same on paper, in 2-D, as she does in real life. If no picture of the model is available, simple test shots – straightforward pictures taken with good lighting and little make-up – can allow you to judge her suitability.

Editorial shoots can take place in studios or on location. Location shoots are powerful as the environment can be chosen to contribute to the image produced; studio shoots are easier to organize. Time on any shoot is limited, so be prepared and equipped to face every eventuality. Consider transport, technical support, access to an electricity and water supply. If you use a public location, check with the local authority if any authorizations are needed. It may be necessary, even in the most benign environment, to guarantee the security of the shoot as well as that of the public. A shoot in a train station, for example, may need to be organized out of peak times. Finally, do not forget to check the weather, and take along extra electrical equipment and lighting, drink, food, a sewing kit and first aid supplies.

Light and shadows contribute significantly to this image by Guillaume Dollinger and Alexandre Fléveau. (See case study on CD)

The idea of layering used by Sean Cabezas in his garment design is extended one step further in this picture through the projection of an image on his model.

PACK SHOT STYLING FOR A LOOK BOOK

In the industry pack shots and **look books** are used as commercial material; they focus on showing the garments, and their styling is often simplified and toned down compared with that of editorial or catwalk. They are usually produced in a studio environment against a plain background. Students find pack shots useful to document their work. Such shoots are easier to organize than editorial ones, but can also be carried out at the same time.

FORMALIZING YOUR STYLING CONCEPT AND SOURCING ACCESSORIES

Having established the financial and practical restrictions that apply to your styling, you now need to formalize your styling concepts for the catwalk, your editorial and look book shoots.

The concept of your collection itself may provide ideas for such styling concepts, but remember that good styling must first of all be compatible with the garments, either in sympathy or contrasting. Use styling concept and mood boards to explain your vision and describe the different elements you want to achieve to the rest of the production team.

Sourcing your accessories can take time and ingenuity. Buy and return is not an option if the article is to be worn, and second hand shops rarely have identical articles in the multiple numbers usually required for the catwalk. There are, however, other ways to get hold of the perfect accessories: you can borrow them, get them sponsored or create them yourself. Bags, jewellery, belts and headwear, such as scarves, hats or wigs, are very effective accessories that can easily be made by any fashion student.

Shoes are an unavoidable element of styling for the catwalk that can prove expensive as you will need a pair per outfit. Do not let poor footwear ruin the effect of your garments. The best solution is often to buy inexpensive shoes and customize them. If successful, such customized accessories will contribute to the expression of a strong style and may be incorporated into your collection. As you gather accessories and props, regularly review your styling by asking a friend to model your outfits and record the fittings by taking pictures.

In all aspects of styling, especially hair and make-up, the quality of execution is important; keep it simple if you are unsure of the quality that can be achieved. Issey Miyake catwalk styling, for example, is often minimalist but very effective. One season, models simply had a helium-filled foil balloon, each of a different colour, attached to the back of their collar that seemed to hover a metre above their heads to great effect. Such effects are easy enough to produce if you can come up with an idea that works with your collection. Styling also requires you to be creative and resourceful.

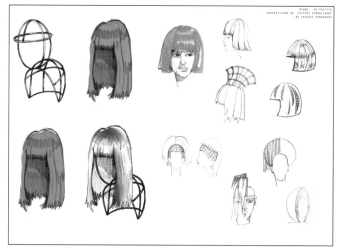

Juliette Alleaume (Atelier Chardon Savard) extended the silhouettes of her outfits with exaggerated wigs.

Sean Cabezas used colourful masks to complete his looks. (See case study on page 176)

Verena Zeller worked with the grammar of her collection to customize shoes. (See case study on page 158)

PRESENTATION FOR SUBMISSION

Depending on their institution, students may have to submit their work on several occasions during the year. Each time a thorough list of the material required will be provided. Overall it is likely to include your garments or toiles but also supporting documentation – your sketchbook, samples, illustrations, theme, concept and mood boards, technical flat drawings and patterns.

Documentation helps the jury to trace the development of each collection, establish the origin of the work and understand its design, but also identify any specific difficulties faced. The jury will be interested to know how you have tackled them. As long as it is authorized by your tutor, you may include any complementary supporting material with your submission that you feel will be useful.

You are unlikely to be present when the jury reviews and grades your work. Your presentation should show your work at its best. By demonstrating good communication skills you will also make the jury's work easier and more pleasant, hence ensuring its goodwill. Make sure that all the material required is included and organized logically. Explain the context of your collection; design can not be evaluated in absolute terms but in relation to its purpose and alongside a brief. This context may be stated partly by your styling but you may also include your personal brief and the work you have done when researching your market, demonstrating you understand your client – the woman you are designing for – and know your competition.

Illustrations and pictures should be selected on their ability to make a point and their coherence with your collection. Their quality and presentation should be professional. Try to include pictures or videos of your garments being worn so that the jury can also appreciate their fit.

Garments, pictures and pattern pieces should be organized so that they can be investigated in your absence and connected with the correct supporting material. Work from different students may get mixed up on the day; references and clear labelling can only help.

To present their work, students are usually allocated a specific exhibition area. Most of the time, you are expected to organize any equipment you may need, from hanging rail to monitors on which to show a video. Presentations should be clean and tidy; even the way you organize your garments on the rail, either by colourway or garment type, will be noticed. But you could go further and create, for example, a house style and merchandise your garments as if they are hanging in a shop with labels, swing tickets and packaging. This is also a form of styling that can demonstrate your understanding of your market.

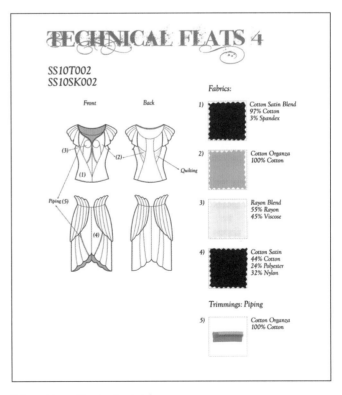

Select with care the visual material you include to explain your collection, whether technical flat (Bernice Chua, above) or illustrations (Andrea Tramontan, left). (See case studies on CD)

MAKING THE MOST OF THE END-OF-YEAR SHOW

The end-of-year fashion show is a unique and exciting opportunity to show your work to a wider public. It is also an important moment for teaching institutions; the year-end show demonstrates the range and quality of their teaching. Prospective students, employers and the press may be invited. Those present will vary according to the environment in which the show takes place. It may be organized with other institutions as part of a student fashion week, or take place within your institution itself. Sometimes, however, if there is no budget available, showing may not be possible.

Students and institutions have the same interests invested in these shows and students will find that helping with their organization can prove an invaluable experience. They may work with their institution to put a show together if none is planned, for instance, or they may help with communication, either sending out invitations or, if the show is part of a larger event, interacting with the public on the stand. Such contributions will not only constitute work experience but will also help you to get in touch with influential people in the industry and target those you want to attend the show and see your work. Who knows – your next employer may be in the crowd. In all your contacts with the industry, be professional and proactive. Find the right angle to approach people and fine-tune your message.

You have worked hard to produce a collection; your garments are made, styled and ready to show. Make the most of this collection and try to see if it can be shown at other fashion events – an alternative fashion week or a young designer's competition, for example. Try to video your garments on the catwalk; this can then be used to advertise yourself and your work on the internet. Finally, make the most of the day. Showing is a unique experience. Be proud of your work and bask in the glory.

Before, during and after the show, backstage organization requires military precision to make the main event on the catwalk appear effortless.

Wrapping Up

Styling is an essential part of fashion. It must be considered as soon as you start garment design and range planning. The way you present your garments and how you style them must contextualize your collection and explain what it is about. It must strengthen the image of your collection and the impact it makes.

This demonstration of your understanding of what constitutes a viable style will help not only your academic achievement but also your search for employment since the styling and documentation of your collection can significantly contribute to your portfolio.

The experience of the past months, designing a capsule collection, will have highlighted the ins and outs of the creative process. Reflect on this experience and try to understand where you have difficulties with the process. See how you can find strategies to resolve them; cultivate what works for you.

After all, there is something magical about designing fashion.

With her final collection, Juliette Alleaume (Atelier Chardon Savard) has developed a strong creative identity that has been widely acknowledged.

EXERCISES IN PROFESSIONAL STYLING

In the last 20 years, staging fashion on the catwalk has become much more creative and sophisticated. Similarly, styling of images has evolved and the expected quality of photography has increased significantly with the development of its technology. Make sure you are aware of these standards. Try to go to shows or watch them on the internet and familiarize yourself with different segments of the fashion media.

BEAUTY

One model and three different looks. These looks have been created to complement the styling of the pack shots, editorial and catwalk.

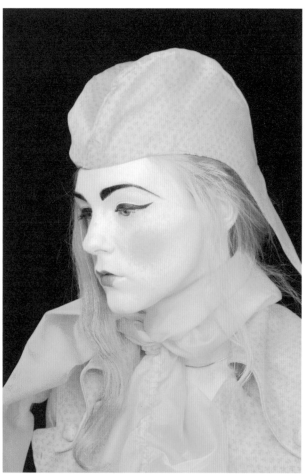

PACK SHOTS

A collection of simple but well-cut silk suits designed by Leony Aneston (Croydon College) are shot in studio conditions for clarity. This showcases the garments' design, detail and cut.

An interesting location can add to
the overall expression, by reflecting,
emphasizing or contrasting with the
spirit of the garments.

By changing the colour to black and
white, resetting the levels of brightness
and contrast, as well as cropping the
images, it is possible to create a totally
different style that can put the garments
into another context.

A collection of mini crinolines, scarves and hats in complementing silk organza has been used to create a stronger style for this suit collection.

This styling gives another dimension to these classic garments – a sense of fun within the serious fit and execution of the pieces.

CHAPTER 7
DIFFUSING YOUR
FINAL COLLECTION

A good portfolio is one that is individual and stands out from the large number design studios usually review. The organization of yours should not follow a formula but express your approach to fashion design and demonstrate your understanding of the industry.

You can organize your portfolio as an art student or artist would do; as an exhibition of your work, its individuality and your creativity. Such an approach usually highlights an interest in a particular style or market. This may be effective if you are applying to become the creative director of an existing label or are looking to raise funds to start your own label.

Alternatively, you can organize your portfolio to demonstrate your versatility and ability to design to a brief – showing that you have the skills required to carry out the job and that you are willing to adapt and understand the market in which you will work. In this case you must review and adapt your portfolio with each job application.

As a graduate you are at a disadvantage compared with professional designers. The academic environment promotes personal and artistic development and students often lose sight of commercial constraints. Your final collection is likely to be the most significant and ambitious body of work you have produced so far and it will represent a large part of your portfolio. You must consider how it reflects on you as a designer and what it says of your ambitions. Your portfolio is likely to be reviewed in your absence; are you confident that it conveys clearly what you intend? Have you, for example, stated the market for your final collection? How does your work relate to the house style of the studio looking to hire? Most of your work is probably over six months old – have you stated when it was designed? How has it aged and how does it stand with current trend forecasts? Is your latest work identifiable?

There is no reason why you should limit the material you include in your portfolio to work produced during your academic training. Fashion ages quickly and so will your designs. Keep working on your sketchbook; this may lead to work and designs you will want to include in your portfolio, not only keeping it fresh but also allowing you to adjust its direction. By maintaining a virtual portfolio on the internet and updating it regularly, you will gain visibility and allow potential employers to follow your development. The internet allows the diffusion of a wide range of material from illustration to videos. However, select the material you show on your site with great care as, unlike a paper portfolio, you cannot customize it according to the people viewing it.

If you are happy with the market targeted by your final collection you could, for example, design for the following season, demonstrating your ability to manage and evolve a given style. Alternatively, you can extend the market reach of your final collection by designing a diffusion range for a different market segment – younger, older, opposite gender, different level of affluence – demonstrating not only your ability to design to a brief but also your understanding of commercial constraints.

WHY DO COMMERCIAL DESIGNERS HAVE SECOND LINES?

Diffusion really is an old trick of the fashion industry – remember the prêt-à-porter collections developed by haute couture houses discussed in Chapter 1? In today's fashion environment diffusion is an essential skill. Through secondary lines fashion labels use the strength of their brand to extend their market reach and access market segments that are usually more price-sensitive and less design-led than their original market.

Such commercial strategies must be coherent; the brand and image of the main line must not be damaged, and the market targeted by the diffusion line must be sensitive to the designer style and brand. Approaches to diffusion vary (branching into accessories or fragrance are two examples), and the purpose may be to quickly increase market share, or perhaps to secure young clients not yet affluent enough to buy the main line. While designers usually diffuse down, others, like Jean Paul Gaultier, who launched his haute couture collection in 1997, move up.

The art of diffusion provides an insight into the commercial reality of fashion and the effects of trends. Maison Martin Margiela, for example, has an extensive range of lines from haute couture to casualwear. Each is designated by a different number: 0+10 and 0 are bespoke men's and women's (haute couture) wear, 10 and 1 prêt-à-porter lines for men and women, 4 women's garments designed for comfort, MM6 women's casualwear, 14 replica vintage garments for men, 22 footwear, 8 eyewear, 11 accessories, 12 fine jewellery, 13 objects and publications, 3 fragrances.

To preserve their image, labels are often unwilling to publicize their commercial strategies to the wider public. To understand their approach to diffusion you must carry out your own research. Some of the garments shown on catwalks and in the press are used mainly for image management. By comparing what was on the catwalk with what is at the point of retail, under the same label or across a diffusion range for a given season, you will develop a sense of what actually sells and how collections are diffused.

These outfits by Alberta Ferretti for her main line (above) and diffusion line, Philosophy, (below) in S/S 2009 are similar in their colour range and silhouettes, but vary in quality of fabric and target market. They are designed with the same spirit.

EXTENDING YOUR FINAL COLLECTION

Designing a secondary line for your final collection does not mean designing a brand new collection but translating your original design for another market, taking into account its specific requirements. If you diffuse down, for example, this market will be wider than the one targeted by your final collection and, therefore, more likely to be affected by trends. You can diffuse your collection in two slightly different ways. In either case your purpose must be explicit and your approach explained and justified.

You can diffuse your collection as it is usually done in the industry: extending its market reach by being more accessible in terms of price and design while maintaining a coherent image and brand. Obviously you must first state the brand image and house style of the label your collection represents.

Alternatively, you may want to demonstrate the versatility of your skills and design garments that could be used by an existing label competing within the market for which you would like to work. In this case you will use your final collection as inspiration to design in the given style of this label. You will need to gain an in-depth understanding of this section of the market, analysing collections, designs and silhouettes as well as communication and marketing strategies.

The way you decide to diffuse your final collection should be guided by the coherence you feel you can maintain between collections as well as the direction you want to give to your portfolio.

It is sometimes possible to produce credible diffusion collections simply by using alternative fabrics as Sintija Reinfelde did with her collection. The pictures above are of the original collection and the ones below are of the diffusion line. (See case study on CD)

PRACTICAL ADVICE

It may be useful to begin the process of diffusion by reconsidering your final collection, adopting an objective point of view. Look at it for what it is, ignoring your knowledge of its development and history. Forget the woman for whom the collection was designed originally and identify afresh the market in which your collection is most likely to succeed, keeping in mind achievable retail prices. From this commercial point of view, re-evaluate what your collection does well and where it is not so successful; identify which garments and elements of design should be removed and those that can be preserved.

Following this analysis, deconstruct the remaining designs in your collection. Imagine how different elements could be reused or transformed into new designs. To this aim you can also revisit the development and sampling stage and the ideas you did not retain.

One key decision you will have to make concerns silhouettes. How do those of your final collection compare with those you forecast for your target market? Can you maintain and exploit those silhouettes, perhaps by simplifying them or by reorganizing some of their lines? Or should you simply abandon them and adopt silhouettes developed by other designers?

You should also consider other aspects of your design and investigate how they could be used or transformed – in particular, materials. Select these according to their cost, ease of care but also the effect they produce. Colour strongly affects the perception of any product and must be adapted to your market. If, like many students in this book, you have produced your own fabric or print, you may think of different ways in which to use these. Certain aspects of your patterns may be reinterpreted or applied in simpler ways. Likewise, some of your embellishments may be simplified and still used for detailing, or transformed into prints. You may be surprised at how easily a collection can be transformed.

You can, if you wish, produce this new range but you might simply illustrate it just as effectively. Explaining its purpose, however, and how it relates both to your original collection and addresses a new market is essential.

Wrapping Up

Fashion design ages quickly and the industry is in a permanent state of flux. The fashion calendar requires a constant flow of designs from professional designers. As a recently graduated student you must adjust to the demands of this new environment. Whether seeking employment or already holding a position, you must keep abreast of new developments in the industry and continue to produce new designs. Updating your portfolio regularly, removing work that does not fit or has aged, freshening up old work or producing new designs will help you steer your development throughout your career.

CASE STUDIES

CATHY AMOUROUX
MECCANO

(École Supérieure des Arts Appliqués Duperré, Paris)

A couture workshop is reminiscent of a construction site, where things are constructed, built, assembled and put together. The origins of my project are to be found in this analogy; it attempts to combine architectural techniques and stylistic codes with those of garment design.

The notion of construction present in both disciplines – garments and edifices – interested me. To illustrate this parallel I designed a collection that is to be built, constructed or deconstructed, and put together by the customer according to their individual taste and imagination.

The garments in my collection are designed to be sold in kits that include pre-cut and perforated elements that can be manipulated and assembled as the customer wishes with screws, rivets and bolts. Depending on their individual creativity and patience each customer can create many different types of garments, from the most simple to the most extravagant.

My project proposes a new construction set, the purpose of which is to put garments together. It offers the tools to the consumer who then becomes the designer.

The concept of architectural construction offered Cathy Amouroux a new vision, leading her to create fashion garments that are original and striking.

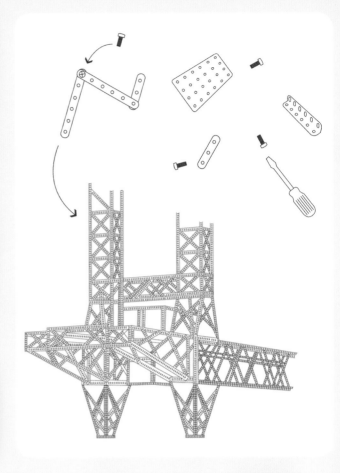

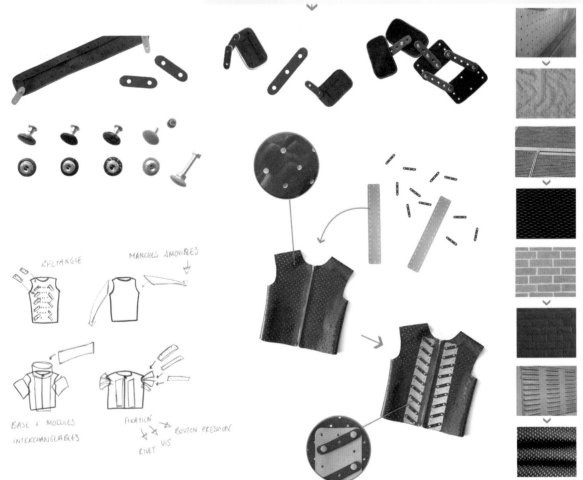

RECTANGLE   MANCHES AMOVIBLES

BASE + MODULES
INTERCHANGEABLES

FIXATION → BOUTON PRESSION
RIVET VIS

Each piece of clothing is broken down into its components so that it can be easily pieced together using rivets and screws.

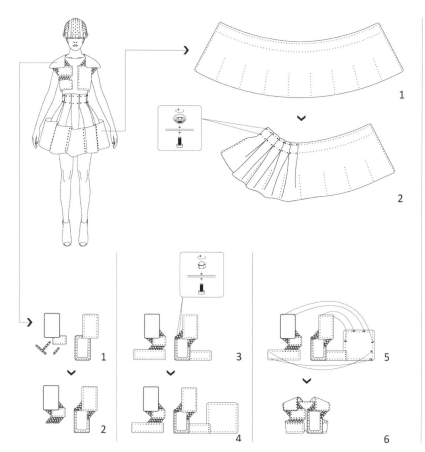

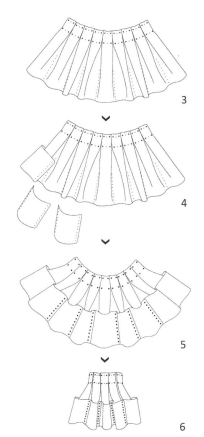

Technical drawings are a vital part of the collection. They show how each piece will be made and the materials required to do so.

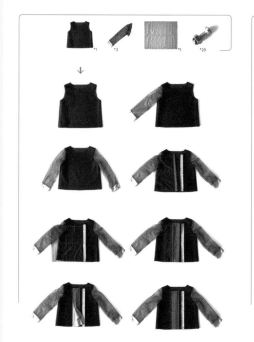

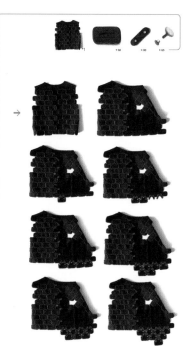

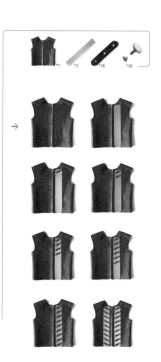

CRISTINA SABAIDUC
ROMANDIN

(Ryerson University, Toronto)

My design ideas are often drawn from ancient history and, in stark contrast, from industrial concepts. The two are then grafted together with innovation and quality workmanship. Romandin's inspirations were the layers in ancient Babylonian engravings and Constant Nieuwenhuys's 'New Babylonian' architectural artwork.

The development phase started with fabric experimentation and colour theory to achieve a better understanding of the abilities and limitations of the materials being used. Silicone caulking and plastic chicken wire were used in conjunction with silks, double knit jerseys and Swarovski crystals.

Romandin was showcased at Ryerson University's annual 'Mass Exodus' graduation show in 2010: 'In Bloom'. The collection was praised for its conscientiousness, wearability and luxury.

Cristina Sabaiduc likes to explore the
unknown, looking for unfamiliar objects,
places and experiences. By combining
the organic colour palette of our natural
environment with products of industrial waste
and overproduction, she creates clothing with
transgressive design concepts that are still
wearable and feminine.

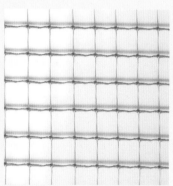

*Silhouettes and design details were roughly
sketched after the fabric development stage,
as opposed to sketching first and assigning
fabrics second. During the making of the
toiles, the colour, form and craftsmanship were
re-evaluated.*

Despite the application of typically strong, masculine, even unattractive materials, Romandin offers pieces with feminine silhouettes, delicate patterns and quality workmanship. In combination with technical drawings and illustrations, the Autumn/ Winter look book assisted in conveying the mood of the collection.

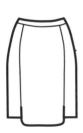

MARILOU DADAT
DRY CLEAN ONLY

(École nationale supérieure des Arts Décoratifs, Paris)

This project began with a fascination for
the atmosphere at a dry cleaners, and many
interconnected images and thoughts formed the
basis of its visual and conceptual inspiration:

Neon lights. White, blue, yellow. A clean
hospital-like light. Coloured papers, stitched
to clean garments, with a bill and a name. The
beauty of an untold dirtiness. Colour is an
accident, a sparkling point in all the beiges and
whites. Plastic wrapping stresses the fragility of
clothing. Garments are wrapped so that they do not
touch each other. In one single room hang tons of
different people's clothes. Tons of clothes with
no flesh in them. What if I want to mix them all?
What if all those colours bleed? Mixing accidents
to create a style.

Garments are named and numbered. Does professional
care mean made with love? Clean shirts ready to go.
I want to unfold them all.

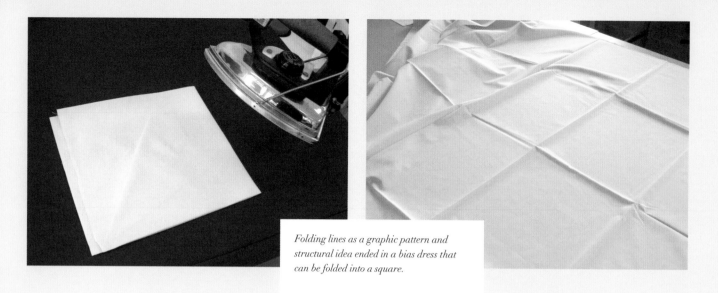

Folding lines as a graphic pattern and structural idea ended in a bias dress that can be folded into a square.

Laundry bags and plastic wrapping provide material inspiration; folding techniques and hangers are used for structural research. The first trials for integrating a hanger shape in cloth.

Finding how a hanger shape can mould a collar. Then adapting the hanger line to a design.

LOOK 1
Stiff 'stitched' leather jacket on plastic coated T-dress.

LOOK 2
Trenchcoat made from a nylon fabric normally used for bags.

LOOK 3
Freshly ironed cocktail dress.

LOOK 5
Working suit inspired.

LOOK 4
'Laundry bag' cocktail dress with a mix of all the collection colours.

LOOK 7
'Laundry bag' wedding dress.

LOOK 6
Folded shirt and 'laundry bag' skirt.

MATTHIEU THOUVENOT
DEATH IN A PINK CLOAK

(Royal Academy of Fine Arts, Antwerp)

My first inspirations were Baroque costumes, ornaments, fabrics, art and colours. I then confronted the extreme richness of these elements with more primal influences – the representation of the Last Judgment or Apocalypse in Christian art, and the medieval crafts. Metalwork from this period inspired the accessories – crowns and jewels – of the collection.

My aim was to build up a structured silhouette, strong yet refined. I was inspired by recent fashions – the couture of the 50s and 60s and its perfect attitude – but also by court costumes and royal attire from the late seventeenth and eighteenth centuries. Fitted cuts and draped volumes, infinite finishings and ornamentation techniques. Materials were chosen according to these historical references; silks of all kinds, sheer organza, strong dupion, structured faille or duchesse... I also decided to work on brocades that I developed myself, from sketching to weaving. This experience allowed me to work on particularly heavy fabrics and bring together mohair wools, cottons, silks and metal yarns. The colour palette is pastel, covering a large range of shades. I worked on total looks of colour. Black has been injected through the collection, starting as hints, ending up totally invading the silhouette.

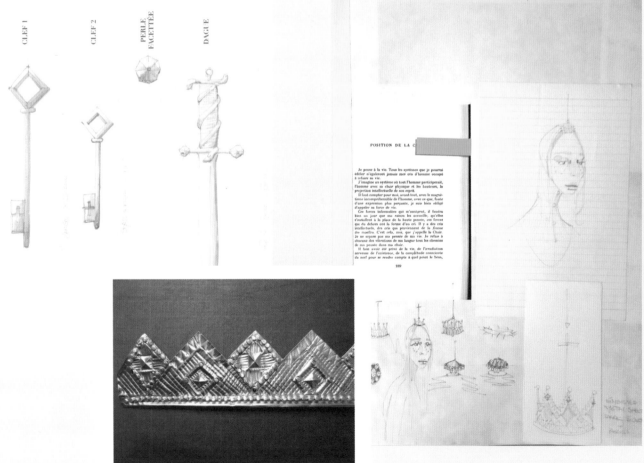

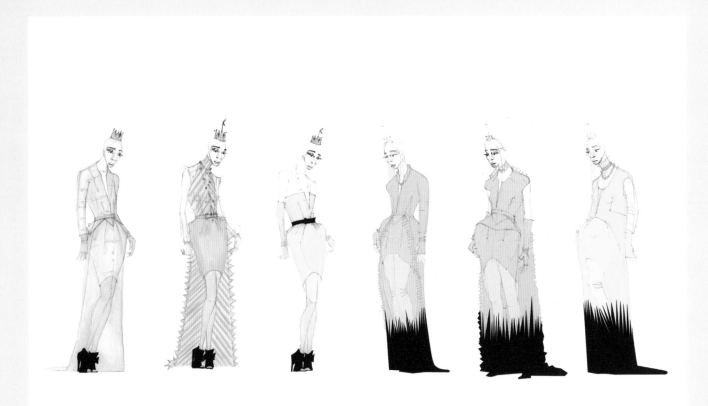

STYLE 05

*White and pink dupion
and organza shirt,
powder satin draped skirt.*

Long wool brocade Deers & Skulls coat, satin skirt and belt, printed brocade slim trousers.

Black and silver Deers & Skulls brocade jacket and skirt, black organza shirt, black velvet belt and gloves.

Bright pink moiré dress and gloves, printed moiré cape, printed taffeta trousers and satin belt.

Long printed brocade cape, dawn faille jacket and gloves, pinstripe taffeta slim trousers.

TINA AILEEN
DI ZECHORI

(Central Saint Martins, London)

```
Di — Disability (inspiration)
Zech — Zecharia (a book from the Bible about
rebuilding the temple or ourselves in terms of
mind and body)
Ori — Origami (method for pattern cutting and the
structure for building the temple)
```

I wanted to design a collection that reflected the personal and spiritual changes I had undergone during my four years at Saint Martins. I had begun to understand others, their personalities, actions and their pasts, and to see the true beauty of other lives.

For me, design must be as fun as playing with toys. I like using simple things as inspiration, so origami was the method I used to make these 'toys'. Origami can transform a 2-D piece into a 3-D shape and curves can be created naturally. I simply 'folded', or draped, my fabric on the body, then made small corrections to it, finally adding fastenings to make a real garment.

My origami method of creating clothes had several benefits. Using the whole of a single piece of fabric meant less waste and lower production costs. It also required less padding and interlining. In addition to using eco-materials and altering old garments to make new pieces, this method enabled me to create ethical designs, and that is something I would like to develop further when designing in the future.

'Amazing Grace, how sweet the sound,
That saved a wretch like me.
I once was lost but now am found,
Was blind, but now I see.'
– John Newton (1725–1807)

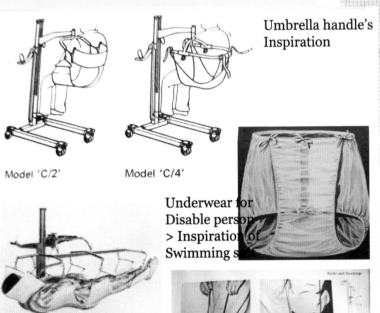

Model 'C/2'   Model 'C/4'

Umbrella handle's Inspiration

Underwear for Disable person > Inspiration of Swimming suit

Stretcher attachment

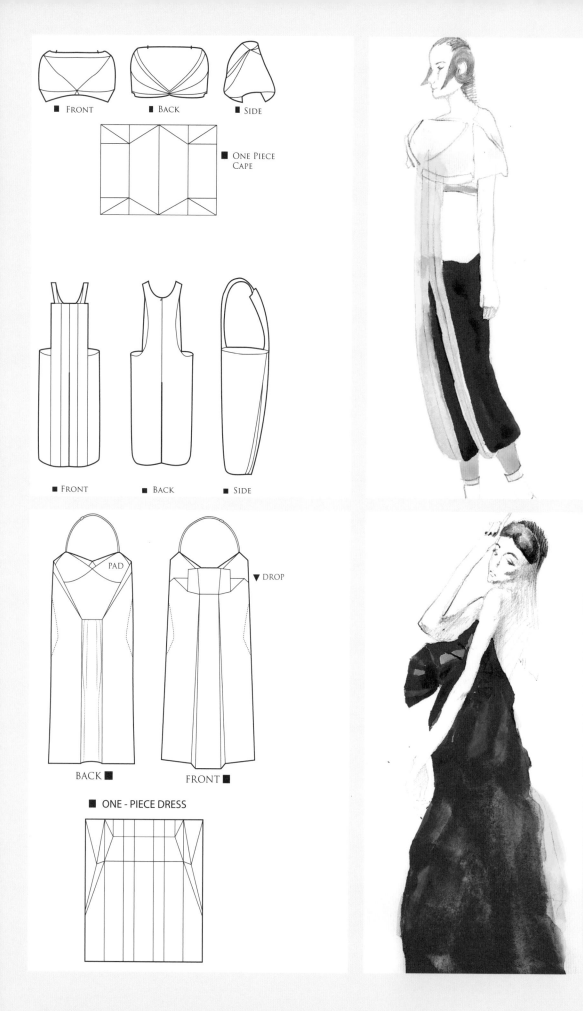

■ Front　　　■ Back　　　■ Side

■ One Piece
　 Cape

■ Front　　　■ Back　　　■ Side

PAD

▼ Drop

BACK ■　　　　　　FRONT ■

■ ONE - PIECE DRESS

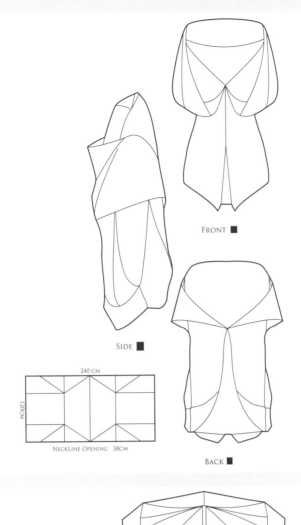

FRONT ■

SIDE ■

240 CM

120CM

NECKLINE OPENING   38CM

BACK ■

■ UMBRELLA
DRESS

■ FRONT

■ SIDE

■ BACK

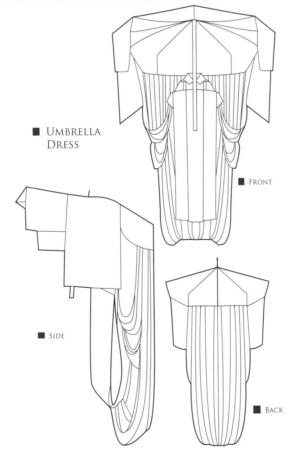

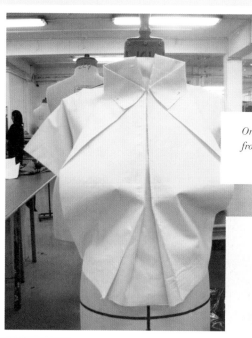

*Origami outfit cut
from just one piece.*

Large-scale origami shirt.

VERENA ZELLER
PALMYRE

(Institute of Fashion Design, Basel)

My collection creates an encounter of yesterday and tomorrow. It is about the zeitgeist of European society in the first decade of the twentieth century. During periods of strict conventions, new movements tend to rise up; old structures degenerate and new forms of art, life and society emerge.

My heroine Palmyre is independent and self-determined. She represents the future vision of women of that epoch before the First World War. Squeezed between the nineteenth century and the modernity of the future, they are looking for a way to express themselves and to strive forward.

A kind of plate tectonics was used as an ideal concept for working the clothes in a modular way. I observed the space inside and outside the garment. The movement in the garment, in addition to the movement of the single pieces when their wearer is walking, was carefully examined. Thus, for every outfit another movement pattern is created.

The wig and shoes complete the look and are a bright and sensual contrast to the very graphic and severe silhouette. The final staging is complete once the garments are placed in the real world, where any backdrop becomes a part of the total look.

Images from Verena's mood board.

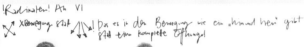

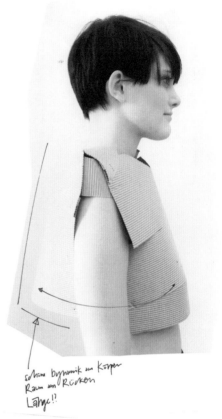

A collage test of
Verena's collection.

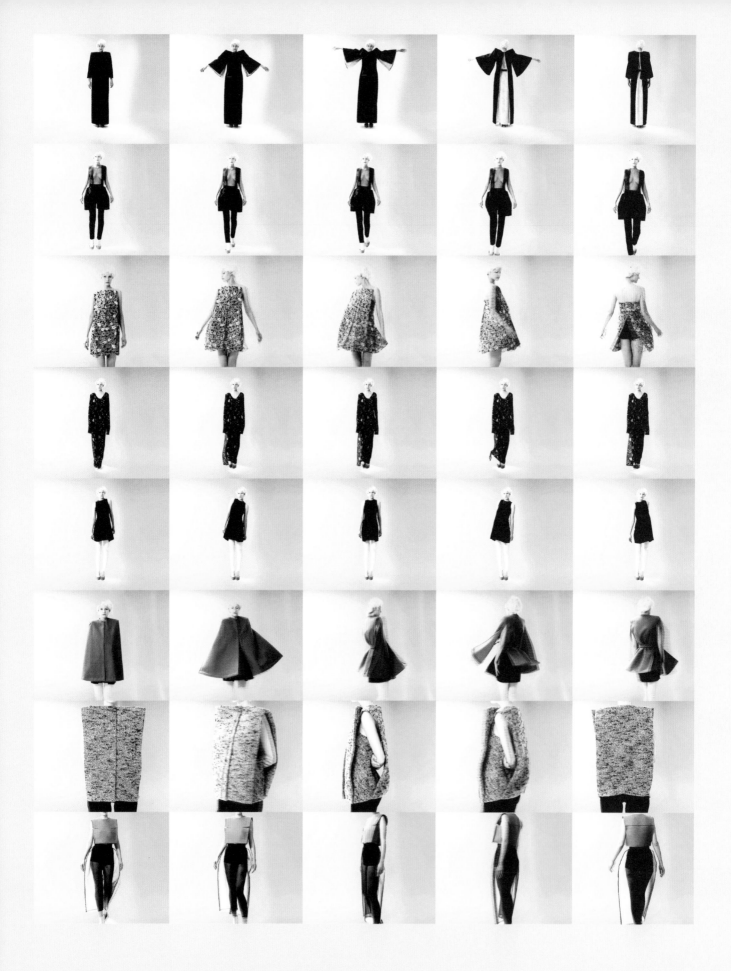

CAMILLE BELLOT
LA VIE RÊVÉE D'UNE FAMILLE DE MONSTRES
(THE DREAM LIFE OF A FAMILY OF MONSTERS)

(Atelier Chardon Savard, Paris)

'My personal space is so sumptuously furnished. If you could only see it, there is such a plethora, and everything is in disorder... Everything moves.' (Dorothea Tanning)

It is from this kind of dimension that the Monster family was born. Monsters from the grandmother through to the last-born – created by repeating the representation of different parts of the human body, moving in a surreal space in which borders disappear and genders reverse.

Can the most bizarre enormity be made real?

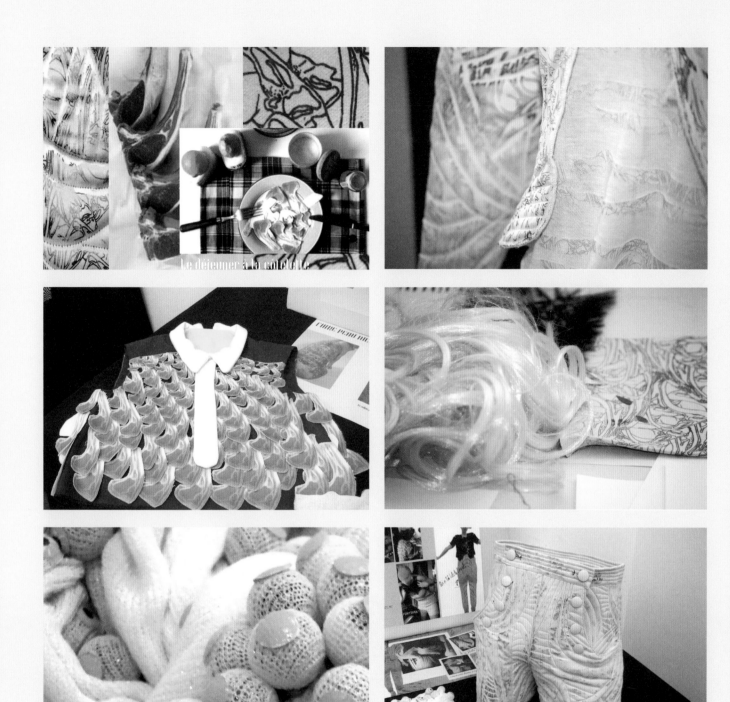

Isolating one element of the body.

Repeating that element.

Deflecting it towards an ornamental
or humorous function.

Camille took inspiration from
Renaissance painters such as
*Lucas Cranach the Elder (*Adam
and Eve) *and Rosso Fiorentino
(*Pietà, *facing page).*

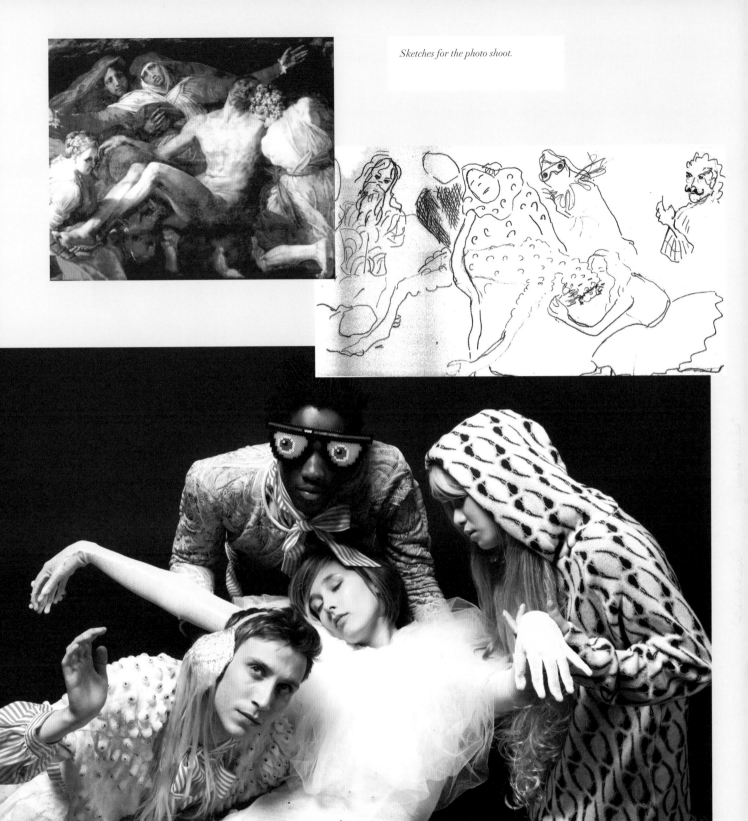

Sketches for the photo shoot.

CLAIRE TREMLETT
THE BEAUTIFUL AND THE OTHER

(University of Wales, Newport)

I began by studying the movement of natural structures and, in particular, a bud unfurling into an extravagant rose. I also wanted to experiment with translating my inspirations directly into textile forms and then into designs. Throughout the design process, I attempted to represent the beauty of nature and to translate its ugly, weird elements into beautiful forms.

My sister was studying to be a surgeon at this time, and I began to consider the one thing our work has in common: stitching. I learnt how to do a surgical stitch and quickly fell in love with the idea of using this slightly vulgar concept for delicate surface detail – again, creating beauty from ugliness.

I also spent a long time looking at insects and shells; their structures, layers and stripy patterns. Returning to a focus on 'the beautiful', I compiled images of orchids, and was inspired by one in particular, the 'Dutchman's Pipe' – its skeletal structure, vivid lime and claret exterior and contrasting purple and white spotted interior, and the way its ornate twisting flesh hangs down. I chose silk organza, silk chiffon and fine wire to replicate this.

During the design process, I drew many extravagant creations, more wearable art than fashion. However, these were eventually scaled back into a final collection that was both wearable and representative of my theme and inspiration.

Claire's creative research encompassed work by Swedish designer Sandra Backlund and Indian designer Manish Arora, amongst others. It also included inspiration from photos and drawings of flowers and in particular, roses.

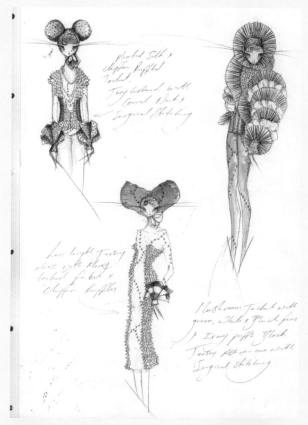

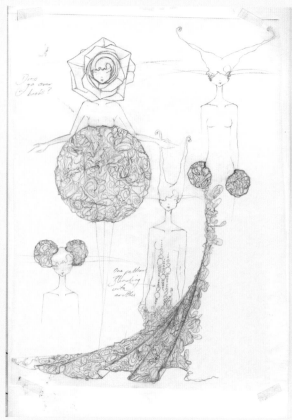

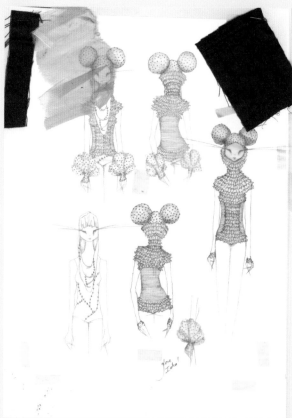

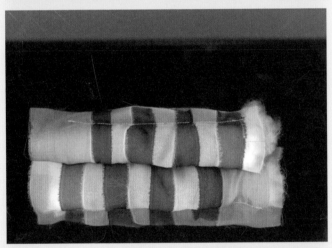

SEAN CABEZAS
CABEZAS ILUMINADAS

(Parsons The New School for Design, New York)

Inspired by the Mexican holiday Día de los Muertos (Day of the Dead), this collection embodies the celebration of one's life. Día de los Muertos is about appreciating the story of your lost loved ones. Taking this idea, I inserted details throughout the entire collection that trigger memories from my past and that have shaped me as a person — from paper masks my father made for me as a child to an outfit that harks back to a Halloween costume I used to love. In the end, this vision was an ode to my family, while giving a glimpse not only into my past but also my future.

The name of Sean's collection, 'Cabezas Illuminadas', is Spanish for 'illuminated heads' and thus refers not only to his surname, but also the jack-o'-lanterns and bright masks worn at Halloween.

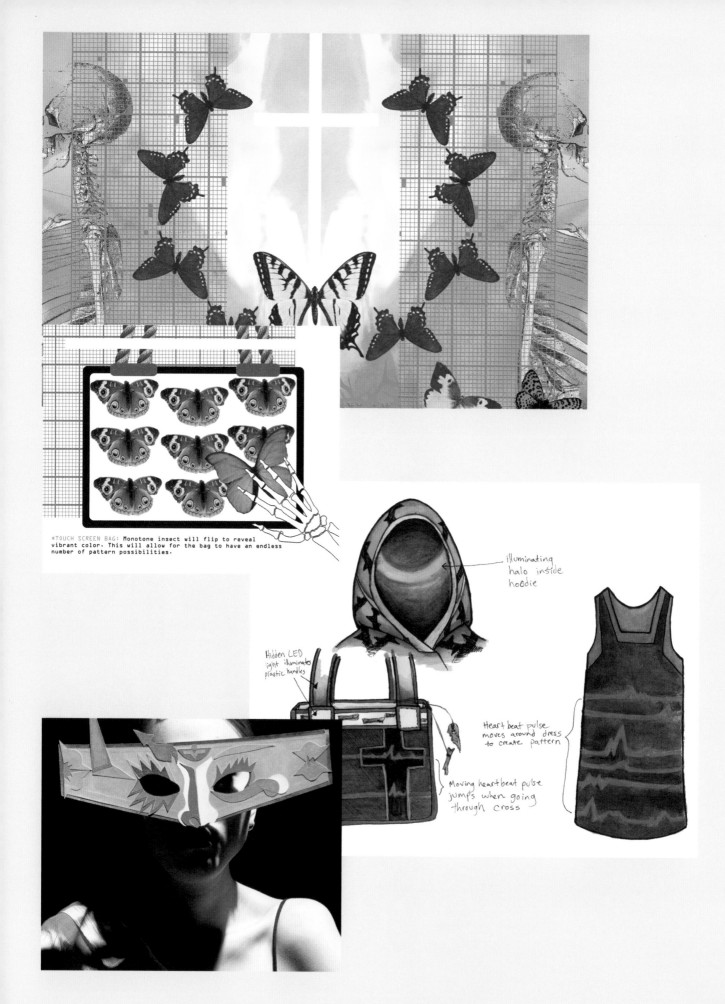

*TOUCH SCREEN BAG: Monotone insect will flip to reveal vibrant color. This will allow for the bag to have an endless number of pattern possibilities.

illuminating halo inside hoodie

Hidden LED light illuminates plastic handles

Heart beat pulse moves around dress to create pattern

Moving heartbeat pulse jumps when going through cross

bubble-up theory
A theory that explains how styles created in the streets by subcultures may find their way into the fashion system and influence the designers usually seen as the creators of style.

calendering
A short-lasting, mechanical fabric finish achieved by pressing fabric at high speed under heat and pressure. This process makes the fabric smoother, more lustrous and sometimes papery. It is used to produce moirés, cambrics and sateens. It is destroyed by washing and in time, by wear.

client board
A visual tool used to explain the target market of the designer. It is often composed of images describing an identity and a lifestyle and it may be used as a source of inspiration.

CMT
An acronym used in the fashion industry when referring to the production of clothing. It stands for Cut, Make and Trim: the three main stages that turn a piece of fabric into a finished garment.

colour forecasting
Usually carried out by **trend forecasters**, colour forecasting tries to anticipate the dominant and popular colours in fashion for a given season.

colour model
These models help identify and reproduce colour precisely. Fashion students are likely to encounter three different models. The RGB model designed for computer screens identifies each colour as a percentage of red, green and blue. The broader-spectrum CMYK model is commonly used by printers and dyers and specifies colours as percentages of cyan, magenta, yellow and black. Finally, the PMS (or Pantone Matching System), a proprietary system, gives each colour an arbitrary reference code. It is used by designers because it has the widest spectrum; each colour reference mixes up to 14 base colours and does not usually come true when converted to another model. Such conversion can only be specified by Pantone or picked from a true Pantone sample.

comp-shop
Short for 'comparative shop', comp-shop is an activity carried out by designers and retailers to evaluate their competition by analyzing what these other suppliers offer their target.

concept
Commonly explained as a 'principle' or an 'idea', 'concept' is synonymous with 'construct'. The concept of a collection is the idea that supports it and explains in what way the garments are unique propositions.

convergent thinking
This is the kind of thinking used to solve a given problem logically. Convergent thinking has a starting point and a conclusion and ideas articulated in between progress step-by-step, converging towards the one correct solution.

crowd funding
This is the pulling together of resources from a large group of people to carry out a specific action, typically disaster relief or political campaigning. Crowd funding is the result of networking or campaigning and has been greatly facilitated by the use of the internet. In fashion, such a process usually involves selling garments before they are made, requiring a minimum volume of sales before being able to deliver.

deconstruction
In fashion design, this term may refer to one of three connected notions: the analysis of a style by teasing apart the different elements that constitute it; the unpicking and reorganization of parts of a garment; a trend popular in the early 1990s for garments with unusual finishes, being either not over-locked or sewn inside-out.

diffusion line
Secondary to the house 'signature line', diffusion lines are usually more commercial and accessible both in terms of cost and design. Diffusions aim to extend the market reach of a label.

divergent thinking
Used to generate ideas, divergent thinking is beneficial to creativity and typically used in brainstorming. It does not attempt to find one correct answer but to produce as many valid propositions as possible.

docket
A term of law in the US, a docket in the UK is a production order that specifies style, fabric, colour, sizing and quantities, maximum unit cost and deadline for delivery to warehouse.

EPOS (electronic point of sale)
Today's cash registers at check-outs are EPOS, electronic points of sale. They register each sale transaction, accounting for payments but also managing rolling stock and informing retailers as to which items sell.

exit
Exits, in a fashion salon or show, refer to a model leaving the catwalk. Before the finale, there is usually one exit for each outfit presented.

fast fashion
This the result of retail practices at the end of the twentieth century whereby the lower cost of garment production and increased reactivity of retail accelerated and shortened fashion trends. Today fast fashion often refers to the fashion sold on the high street; perceived as throw-away fashion, it is seen as socially and environmentally damaging.

filament yarn
This is produced by light spinning of long strands of fibre, usually silk or man-made. It differs from

spun yarn that is produced by higher spinning of shorter fibres. Filament yarns have the regularity required for smooth and lustrous materials such as organza and satin.

fit line
This is the result of the joining of different pieces of cloth cut in shapes designed to create fit and form. When highlighted by the design it is also a **style line**.

grand couturier
A French expression that translates as 'great dressmaker' and refers to fashion designers who create haute couture. The status of grand couturier is traditionally seen as the highest in fashion.

grey state
This is the condition of fibre, yarn or cloth when prepared for dying.

haute couture
A legally protected label, governed by its union, the Chambre Syndicale de la Haute Couture in Paris. It requires that designers present two collections a year in Paris and that they make garments to order, with at least one client fitting. Haute couture is considered the ultimate in garment design because of the range of skills and techniques it relies upon.

injection
The design, production and delivery, through an accelerated process (as short as 12 days) of a few garment designs to answer a customer demand that is not satisfied by the main collection. Only large high street retailers are able to carry out this practice.

intelligent/smart fabrics
Fabrics developed to produce garments that improve the comfort and safety of their wearer, sometimes through monitoring of the person and their surrounding. Gore-Tex, able to let moisture flow only from the inside out, is the most common smart fabric. Intelligent/smart fabrics usually rely on nanotechnologies that provide very specific qualities to the material or on a combination of electronic and conductive material able to monitor vital signs (Adidas's Numetrex sport-bra, for example, is designed to measure its wearer's heart rate).

look book
Used to present the work of models, photographers or designers and fashion labels, look books are commercial tools that focus on the garments presented. They usually relying on studio pictures with limited styling, also known as **pack shots**.

mercerization

A chemical finish applied to cotton or hemp, in the form of thread or fabric, to increase its lustre. Treating these fibres with sodium hydroxide modifies the cellulose structure, resulting in a swelling that increases reflectance and softness.

mood board

These usually consist of a combination of tactile and 3-D elements and of images and pictures that express the feeling and the mood of a collection.

overdyeing

The process of dyeing fabric not in a **grey state**, hence already dyed. For best effect, overdyeing must use a colour darker than the original one, which however sometimes remains somewhat visible.

pack shot

Photography presenting products as seen by customers, hence often includes packaging and labelling. In fashion design, pack shots are studio pictures with little styling, usually gathered into a **look book** to present a collection.

ply yarn

Yarn produced by twisting together several threads or ply.

prêt-à-porter

A French expression translated as 'ready-to-wear'. In English it refers only to ready-to-wear designed by **haute couture** houses, usually produced by external manufacturers to a standard house fit.

range plan

The organization and presentation of the garments that constitute either a collection or a retail stock. In the case of retail, range plans focus on optimizing sales and specify volumes of stocks for garments organized according to type, style, colour and size.

salon

A French word today commonly referring to trade fairs and exhibitions. In fashion it may also refer to fashion fairs or to the room where designers present their collections to a limited audience.

sealed sample

A finished garment produced by a factory to demonstrate a level of quality and finish. It has a contractual value and is used as a reference to evaluate the quality of the **docket** produced.

signature

This is a style easily and commonly identified as originating from an individual, a designer or a label. Burberry's tartan is its signature.

silhouette

The outline of a shape, in fashion of an outfit. Silhouettes are very important in fashion as they are usually the first aspect of a style to be perceived.

single spun yarn

A yarn produced by spinning fibre, not by twisting together threads or ply.

spun yarn

A yarn produced by spinning short fibres in order for them to hold together. It is different from **filament yarn**, produced by lighter spinning of longer fibres. Spun yarns make soft, warm and light fabrics.

story

This refers, in fashion merchandising, to the organization of stock garments into outfits to be presented on the shop floor. Creating stories is one aspect of **styling**.

style line

Usually a **fit line**, the result of the joining of different pieces of cloth cut in shapes designed to create fit and form, highlighted for aesthetical purposes.

styling

The activity of combining garments into looks, usually includes choice of model, hairstyle, make-up and accessories but may extend further to music, set design etc. Styling is central to the presentation of fashion.

theme board

A board presenting a selection of inspirational images (and text), usually based around one or two themes that aid designers to generate design ideas during the development and sampling stage.

toile

The prototype of a garment design, called a muslin in the United States and Canada and referring to the inexpensive material used for that purpose. Such material however must have qualities, in particular weight and handle, similar to that of the intended final fabric.

TPI (turns per inch)

Fibres are spun to hold together and produce yarn. With that aim, fibres of different lengths require different levels of spin as indicated by the TPI or turns per inch. From 2 to 12 TPI produces soft-twist yarns, soft and flexible. From 20 to 30 TPI produces hard twist yarns, firm and crimped.

trend forecaster

A person who usually works as part of a large team that filters through a vast array of information to try and identify, two seasons ahead, the ideas and aesthetics that will influence customers' behaviour and result in fashion trends.

trickle-across theory

A term derived from the trickle-down theory and referring to the idea that styles developed in different creative fields and fashion markets influence each other.

trickle-down theory

A theory that explains how a fashion style introduced by fashion designers increases in popularity as it is adopted by successive groups of people to become mainstream.

warp yarn

The yarn that runs in the length of a piece of cloth. During weaving warp yarns are held in tension on a frame or a loom.

weft yarn

The yarn drawn through the warp yarns during weaving. Because it is not stretched on the loom, the weft (or woof) yarn does not need to be as strong as the yarn used for the warp.

window dressing

An expression that refers to the presentation in shop windows of garments selected for their impact. In fashion design, window dressing qualifies outfits identified for their visual strength rather than their commercial potential. They are used to promote a strong image and attract media attention.

yarn count

A number inversely proportional to the weight of a fabric. An 800-count cotton, for example, is twice as light as a 400-count cotton. This relationship, however, does not hold across fibres, each having a different scale. The metric yarn count represents the length of yarn in kilometres necessary to produce a kilogram of fabric.

FURTHER READING

GENERAL

Jenkyn Jones, Sue. *Fashion Design*, Laurence King Publishing, 3rd edition, 2011.

Posner, Harriet. *Marketing Fashion,* Laurence King Publishing, 2011.

CONTEXT AND HISTORY

Barnard, Malcolm. *Fashion Theory: A Reader,* Routledge Student Readers 2007.

Frisa, Maria Luisa. *Italian Fashion Now,* Marsilio, 2011.

Fukai, Akiko and Barbara Vinken, Susannah Frankel, Hirofumi Kurino, et al. *Future Beauty: 30 Years of Japanese Fashion,* Merrell Publishers, 2010.

Fukai, Akiko. *Fashion History: A History from the 18th to the 20th Century,* Taschen 25th anniversary edition, 2006.

Laver, James and Amy de la Haye, *Costume and Fashion: A Concise History,* Thames & Hudson, 4th edition, 2002.

Saillard, Olivier and Guy Marineau, *Histoire idéale de la mode contemporaine: Les plus beaux défilés de 1971 à nos jours*, Textuel, 2009.

Wilcox, Claire. *The Golden Age of Couture: Paris and London 1947–1957,* V & A Publishing, 2008.

Worsley, Harriet. *Decades of Fashion,* Konemann UK Ltd, 2006.

DRAWING FOR FASHION

Donovan, Bil. *Advanced Fashion Drawing: Lifestyle Illustration,* Laurence King Publishing, 2010.

Peacock, John. *The Complete Fashion Sourcebook: 2,000 Illustrations Charting 20th-Century Fashion*, Thames & Hudson, 2005.

Riegelman, Nancy. *9 Heads: A Guide to Drawing Fashion,* 9 Heads Media, 3rd edition, 2006.

Szkutnicka, Basia. *Technical Drawing for Fashion*, Laurence King Publishing, 2010.

Wesen Bryant, Michele. *Fashion Drawing: Illustration Techniques for Fashion Designers,* Laurence King Publishing, 2011.

ELEMENTS OF DESIGN

Albers, Josef. *Interaction of Color,* Yale University Press, 2006.

Bowles, Melanie and Ceri Isaac. *Digital Textile Design*, Laurence King Publishing, 2009.

Cohen, Allen C. and Ingrid Johnson and Joseph J. Pizzuto. *Fabric Science,* Fairchild, 9th edition, 2009.

Hallett, Clive and Amanda Johnston. *Fabric for Fashion: A Comprehensive Guide to Natural Fibres*, Laurence King Publishing, 2010.

Itten, Johannes. *The Art of Color: The Subjective Experience and Objective Rationale of Color,* John Wiley & Sons, 2nd edition, 1974.

Joseph-Armstrong, Helen. *Draping for Apparel Design,* Fairchild Books, 2nd revised edition, 2008.

———. *Patternmaking for Fashion Design,* Pearson Education, 5th edition, 2009.

Nakamichi, Tomoko. *Pattern Magic*, Laurence King Publishing, 2010.

———. *Pattern Magic 2*, Laurence King Publishing, 2011.

———. *Pattern Magic: Stretch Fabric*, Laurence King Publishing, 2012.

Shaeffer, Claire B. *Couture Sewing Techniques,* Taunton Press Inc, new edition, 2001.

Wolff, Collette. *The Art of Manipulating Fabric,* KP Books, 2nd edition, 1996.

INDEX

PICTURE CREDITS

Grateful acknowledgement is extended for the use of the following images. Every effort has been made to trace all copyright holders. The publisher apologizes for any unintentional omission or error and will be pleased to insert the appropriate acknowledgement in any subsequent edition of the book.

p. 8 Istituto Marangoni fashion show photograph by Mark Atkinson.
p. 13 Winchester School of Art fasion show photograph by Ken Kajoranta.
pp. 18 and 19 Jean-Paul Gaultier © catwalking.com
p. 20 Vivienne Westwood © Niall McInerney; Comme des Garçons © catwalking.com; Versace © Niall McInerney
p. 21 Emporio Armani © UPPA/Photoshot; IKKS courtesy of IKKS; Anne Taylor © WWD/Condé Nast/Corbis
p. 22 Kate Moss/Topshop © CARL DE SOUZA/AFP/Getty Images; Biba © 2006 Topfoto
p. 23 Adidas © Chris Weeks/Wireimage/Getty Images
p. 24 Chanel © Anthea Simms Photography; Chantal Thomass © PIERRE VERDY/AFP/Getty Images
p. 25 Missoni © Antonio Calanni/AP/Press Association Images
p. 28 Prada © catwalking.com
p. 29 Prada © FILIPPO MONTEFORTE/AFP/Getty Images
p. 30 Viktor & Rolf courtesy of Victor & Rolf / Photography by Peter Stigter
p. 32 Alexander McQueen © Anthea Simms Photography
p. 33 Bergdorf Goodman window © Erik Pendzich/Rex/Rex Features
p. 34 Fashion week © Niall McInerney
p. 35 Sienna Miller @ Andy Butterton/PA Archive/Press Association Images
p. 36 Burberry © Hulton-Deutsch Collection/CORBIS; Katharine Hepburn © Keystone Archives/HIP/Topfoto; 1953 raincoat © Chaloner Woods/Getty Images; Aquasprite © Jamie Hodgson / Getty Images
p. 37 Christian Dior 1975 © Keystone/Getty Images; Antony Price 1988 © catwalking.com; Ralph Lauren 1996 © catwaking.com
p. 38 1960s fashion © Cultura Creative/Alamy; Niemeyer architecture © Ludovic Maisant/Hemis/Corbis
p. 39 Chanel © Niall McInerney
p. 40 Mudpie colour palette courtesy of Mudpie
p. 41 Christopher Kane courtesy of Christopher Kane; Giles Deacon © Anthea Simms Photography; Erdem © catwalking.com
p. 43 MPDClick screengrabs courtesy of Mudpie
p. 44 HCP moodboards courtesy of HCP; Mudpie moodboard courtesy of Mudpie
p. 45 Dolce & Gabbana S/S 2011© Anthea Simms Photography
p. 46 Rodarte A/W 2011 courtesy of Rodarte
p. 48 Yohji Yamamoto © catwalking.com; Calvin Klein © News (UK) Ltd/Rex Features
p. 59 Lucy Orta courtesy of Studio Orta
p. 60 photograph of the Eiffel Tower by the author
p. 69 Clements Ribeiro courtesy of Modus Publicity; Custo Barcelona S/S 2011 collection courtesy of XXL Comunicacion (Custo Barcelona); Prabal Gurung © catwalking.com
p. 73 Jeremy Laing courtesy of Jeremy Laing
p. 74 (top) Pesi Girsch, Natures Mortes, courtesy of Pesi Girsch
p. 81 Cristobal Balenciaga © Mary Evan Picture Library 2008; Balenciaga by Nicolas Ghesquière © catwalking.com
p. 82 Roland Mouret © catwalking.com
p. 85 (bottom) Victor & Rolf courtesy of Victor & Rolf / Photography by Philip Riches
p. 92 Hussein Chalayan © catwalking.com; Claude Montana © catwalking.com
p. 94 Valentino © Niall McInerney
p. 100 John Galliano © Niall McInerney
p. 101 ISSEY MIYAKE EUROPE A/W 2011 courtesy of ISSEY MIYAKE / Photography by Frédérique Dumoulin
p. 114 Croydon College fashion show photography by Mark Hodge.
p. 123 Alberta Ferretti courtesy of Alberta Ferretti

ADDITIONAL CREDITS FOR STUDENT DESIGN WORK

(in order of appearance)

Verena Zeller/Institute of Fashion Design, Basel: photography by Benjamin Hofer; modelling by Caroline Weps, Myriam Marti, Barbara Wegmann, Maria Baer, Anja Thomer, Ksenia Yakhontova.

Tina Aileen/Central Saint Martins College of Art and Design, London: photography: Lisa Marie Standbridge; modelling by Victoria Niranath at M& P models; hair/make-up by Ingrid Delarue.

Kai Ryosuke/Musashino Art University, Tokyo.

Claire Tremlett/University of Wales, Newport: photography by Ken Kajoranta; modelling by Bethany Kirkpatrick at M&P models; hair/make-up by Ingrid Delarue.

Bernice Chua/Lasalle College of the Arts, Singapore: photography by Chuck Reyes; modelling by Alisa Mikhaylova.

Cathy Amouroux/Ecole Supérieure des Arts Appliqués Duperré, Paris: photography by Thomas Knights; modelling by Cassie at Select Model Management, London: styling by Sasha Rainbow; make-up by Afron Radojicic; hair by Shinya Fukam.

Camille Bellot/Atelier Chardon Savard, Paris: photography by Sacha Héron and Cédric Bosquet.

Matthieu Thouvenot/Royal Academy of Fine Arts, Antwerp: photography by Zeb Daemen; modelling by Helene at IMM Bxl; hair/make-up by Els Van Schoor.

Andrea Tramontan/Università Iuav di Venezia, Venice: photography by Francesco De Luca; modelling by Francesca Bertini.

Valentine Cloix/Ecole nationale supérieure des Arts Décoratifs, Paris: photography by Hugo Mapelli; modelling by Alicia Noerg; make-up by Davile Babraviciute.

Dez Bara/Ryerson University, Toronto: photography by Lynsie Roberts.

Guillaume Dollinger and Alexandre Fléveau/Ecole Supérieure des Arts Appliqués Duperré, Paris: photography by Joe Boggon; modelling by Anna Saminina at Next Model agents, Paris and Florent Sobczak at Bananas Mambo, Paris.

Cristina Sabaiduc/Ryerson University, Toronto: photography by Calvin Yan and Angela Y. Martin; modelling by Deirdre Buryk and Janel Fordon.

Katya Babenko/Omsk Design School, Omsk: photography by Irina Skabelkina; modelling by Anastasia Yudova.

Mariel Manuel/Royal Academy of Fine Arts, Antwerp: photography by Valentina Vos, modelling by Sara Lucassen; make-up by Annelien Debusschere.

Janosch Mallwitz/Universität der Künste, Berlin: photography by Magdalena Lepka and Corina Leccav.

Sean Cabezas/Parsons, The New School for Design, New York: photography by Alexander Ho and Stephanie Yang; modelling by Shantae Molina; make-up by Oscar Reyes; accessories photography by Oscar Reyes.

Sophie Willett/Central Saint Martins College of Art and Design, London: photography by Sophie Willett.

Sintija Reinfelde/Croydon College of Art, London: photography by Lisa Marie Stanbridge and Catwalk Capture; modelling by Sophie Wilkinson at M&P Models; hair and make-up by Ingrid Delarue.

Tsolo Munkh/Atelier Chardon Savard, Paris: photography by Rémy Lamande, Yannis Vlamas and Tsolo Munkh.

Juliette Alleaume/Atelier Chardon Savard, Paris.

Irene Corazza/Università Iuav di Venezia, Venice: photography by Francesco De Luca; modelling by Francesca Bertini.

Tatyana Kobikova/Omsk Design School, Omsk: photography Nikolia Rozdestvenskiy; modelling by Anatasia Karabnova and Dasha Bichevina.

Lucy Zhang/Jiangnan University, Wuxi: photography by Xuan Gu; modelling by Xiang Ji, Yixuan Wang, Ziyan Zhou, Xini Feng and Lingyun Han.

Marilou Dadat/Ecole nationale supérieure des Arts Décoratifs, Paris: photography by Benjamin Fanni; modelling by Chloe Loughnan – booked by Sam Tirloy at Crystal Models Group; hair/make-up by Gaelle Bertoletti.

Leony Aneston/Croydon College of Art, London: photography by Lisa Marie Stanbridge; modelling by Sophie Wilkinson; hair/make-up by Ingrid Delarue.

Verity Pemberton/Winchester School of Art, Southampton: photography by Valerie Phillips; modelling by Camilla Babbington.

ABOUT THE PARTICIPATING SCHOOLS

Atelier Chardon Savard, Paris

Atelier Chardon Savard, Paris, was founded in 1988 by Dominique Savard and Cyrille Chardon with the intention of training a limited number of fashion designers able to achieve recognition in the industry. The skills acquired during the students' first years, including illustration, colour theory, draping and modelling, trends and market analyses, all contribute to the successful production, in the fourth and final year, of a collection based on an individual concept.

There is some truth in the expression 'talent cannot be learned'; a methodology specific to the creative process, however, can be taught. The birth of a creative identity is always a triumph; our objective is to participate and assist in this process. The creative act relies on seemingly contradictory intellectual abilities: to take risk and walk the tight rope without fear, to use intuition without moderation but carry out analysis rigorously and to show immense ambition as well as total modesty. This back and forth between inductive and deductive reasoning, from global to sequential and from perception to translation is the focus of the Atelier's attention; for balance is delicate and desire volatile. Observing these adventures, we have identified successive stages: inspiration, research, realization and production.

Inspiration requires a magpie's curiosity, abundant and varied information but also introspection and the identification of connections linking these disparate materials – all in order to fuel the fire that must sustain the following research stage. Research can be long, exciting, risky, unnerving and sometimes discouraging. Often it is the most difficult stage but it is at the core of the process. It's often at this time, that a transgression, the most improbable and unexpected result of experimentation occurs and that triumphs the confirmation of 'the idea'. Once the fever has broken, then perspective, verification of the hypothesis, restraint and realization must follow. Selection of appropriate materials along with pattern making and production skills and techniques, all guarantee a faithful translation. The final step sees the creation of a scenario, the choice of models, fittings and music, and the construction of a visual communication.

Bath Spa University, Bath

The course at Bath Spa was conceived by fashion professionals eager to introduce a brand new entity into design education: a programme written and delivered by a team directly from industry, for industry, focussing on the 'traditional' skills of fashion design while encouraging the development of creativity, personal identity and vision.

It is our philosophy that to design effectively designers need a thorough understanding of the technical aspects of fashion. We therefore focus on developing and interpreting ideas in 3-D, the fundamental artform of the designer. We felt graduates were losing the art of being able to process their ideas within a studio, or communicate ideas to a sample factory or team because they had limited experience of exploring ideas outside of 2-D. The great designers are all master pattern-cutters, and to understand design fully we believe all designers have to master this skill, understand what they are sketching in terms of cut, silhouette, proportion, finish and design detail, as well as be able to effectively translate the ideas into 3-D and show a good use of colour and fabric.

The theoretical side of fashion is key to understanding and with this in mind we developed a unique partnership with the Fashion Museum in Bath, offering a fully integrated programme of lectures, as well as the fantastic opportunity and privilege to use the vast museum archives for research.

Fashion students work in a small and intimate studio setting not dissimilar to that of a traditional atelier. The daily hub of activity in the studios, with endless toiling of ideas, experimenting creatively with shape and form, and carrying out fittings, is a joy to watch. This practical expertise mixed with a good understanding of the more commercial areas of the fashion industry, good research and drawing skills, and above all good communication, should prepare graduates for the realities of a demanding, yet fabulous career within fashion.

Berlin University of the Arts / Universität der Künste, Berlin

Clothing involves people; it is a (design) language that contributes to a collective memory and expresses a period in time. While specific clothing may or may not be associated to a particular moment in history, it is always the result of distinct societal, political and design developments.

The role of fashion designers is to produce garments that are groundbreaking expressions of their own time, thereby contributing to it, shaping it. Capturing this expression within an object is a strategic task; it must be purposefully planned and clearly articulated. A random approach to this process may weaken the artistic credibility, and thus the conceptual added-value, of the resulting product.

Defining, developing and portraying convincingly the personal expression of this conceptual added-value is the focus of the fashion designer curriculum at the Universität der Künste (UdK). The design process at UdK offers a framework for dealing with various topics within the subject studied, as well as interdisciplinary links to other subjects.

In contrast to teaching methods at some colleges and private institutions, students at UdK are not expected to adapt a predefined design language. Rather, the entire design process, from research and brainstorming to presentation, is regarded as an experimental, non-standardized project that must be carried-out utilizing the highest level of technical, technological and scientific principles.

The diversity and quality of the teaching and workshops in our course of study, as well as the possibility of interdisciplinary cooperation are essential to achieve this. Goal-oriented, experimental work requires a broad base of knowledge as well as subject-specific specialization.

This type of teaching enables our graduates to conduct well-founded research, to think and draw conclusions in an interdisciplinary manner, to define quality, and to find and convey their own artistic expression. All of these are skills that must be learned and experienced by fashion designers.

Central Saint Martins College of Art and Design, London

Fashion is a fast moving and highly diverse international industry encompassing a wide range of markets and creative, production and communication practices. It also has historical and social significance for our understanding of some of the important values that underpin our culture. Recognition of this diversity and cultural meaning is central to the course's rationale and structure. By helping you develop appropriate intellectual and practical skills, the course enables you to benefit from such diversity and to rise to the challenges it presents.

The course's philosophy is to create a learning environment in which innovation and originality are nurtured within a range of different but closely related pathways. We aim to produce versatile fashion specialists able to solve problems creatively while drawing on a deep knowledge of their chosen fields and a critical understanding of the social, economic and cultural factors influencing their professional environment.

The course offers a choice of seven pathways: Fashion Design Menswear, Fashion Design Womenswear, Fashion Print, Fashion Design with Knitwear, Fashion Communication with Promotion, Fashion Design with Marketing, Fashion History and Theory. With the study of fashion as their core subject, these options represent a uniquely synergistic combination of fashion design, communication, historical studies and theoretical studies led by tutors who are expert practitioners. The pathway range allows you to study a specific area of fashion practice in depth, embracing different approaches to the subject and a range of creative opportunities within the industry.

Croydon College, London

The three-year fashion design course offered at Croydon College is organized to allow the development of the students' technical skills, in particular pattern cutting and CMT and the exploration and expression of their creativity in garment design.

From their first trimester onwards, students are taught through projects of increasing complexity the basic skills of research, design, pattern cutting and construction. This project-based work is complemented with additional experience of industrial practices including hands-on use of the 'Gerber pattern cutting system'.

With this two years training, students are equipped, in their third year, to work on the design, production and presentation of their capsule collection, intended to round up their skills and demonstrate their creative and technical abilities. Each student identifies and researches the market in which they feel they would prefer to work. They then are encouraged to find the necessary influences and inspiration to create and design a suitable collection.

Research and development and garment design are two vital stages of the process at Croydon College where students can concretely and practically express their creativity relying on 2- and 3-D creative pattern cutting techniques. With constant mentoring by the staff, students are encouraged to allow themselves the freedom to break down the confines of today's designs and re-build the idea of tomorrow without losing sight of the reality and commercial aspect required to survive in today's world of fashion.

Ecole Supérieure des Arts Appliqués Duperré, Paris
It is not an easy task to articulate the approach to designing a fashion collection that is favoured at Duperré: we consider that each of our students travels an individual journey. Each creative project, however, must follow a rational methodology.

The first stage, the formulation of the concept of the project is vital; it articulates the basic syntax of the collection. Sources, documents, notions, concepts … they are signifiers that must be gathered, structured and articulated in a compelling discourse to be translated into a fashion collection. In this regard, we consider that a radical point of view may be expressed in garments and accessories because fashion is a vehicle for meaning, a vector of signs.

After this work of semantic structuring, crystallisation into products follows: the transformation of a project into a collection of garments and accessories. To this end, we identify with the students, partners in the industry and the school (firms and workshops) that may collaborate on their individual collection. This requires the students properly articulate the foundations of their projects: the know-how, technologies, contexts, encounters and experiences that will help them towards the creation of their products. Our training highlights the importance of such professional collaborations and confirms the future designers as mediators between various stakeholders and as artistic director of their own work.

It is as such that they must address the commercial and technical viability of their products. The resulting choices determine a marketing approach. Step by step a collection takes shape, shifting and changing until its fulfilment. Finally the project is wrapped within a strong visual identity and the students must propose a contextualized presentation of their collections (including, packaging, production of visuals, merchandising...).

Together these different stages (and many more inherent to each individual project) constitute the adventure of a collection and prepare the students for their future professional lives.

Ecole nationale supérieure des Arts Décoratifs, Paris
At the Ecole nationale supérieure des Arts Décoratifs (EnsAD) garments are considered as much more than items of clothing and it is understood that their existence extends beyond their design. Their creation must be multidisciplinary and call upon technical skills, artistic reasoning, prospective analysis, understanding of industry structures and of the markets.

Four approaches to fashion are identified: garment design that favours a functional approach and innovation, 'stylisme' or fashion design concerned with style rather than function, costume design that creates garments specific to performance arts and finally accessories, from hats and bags to perfume bottles.

Up to the second year of their five-year curriculum, Ecole nationale supérieure des Arts Décoratifs students, admitted after a taxing selection process (80 to 85 admissions for 2500 applications), follow the same general curriculum designed to prepare them to one of ten decorative art specialities: product design, textile design, fashion design, multimedia/graphic design, printed images, photography/video, animation, spatial art, interior design, stage design. Ecole nationale supérieure des Arts Décoratifs aims to train creative designers capable of inventing new means of expression – from conception to production – and of finding answers to questions posed by our society.

Specialization in fashion design starts in the second year with an extensive training in material and colour theory. The third and fourth years see an increasing level of specialization and project work with a focus on technology. Explorations of traditional techniques as well as the most advanced technologies are made possible thanks to the school's strong links with the industry and the high quality of its laboratories. Students at Ecole nationale supérieure des Arts Décoratifs have the opportunity and are encouraged to collaborate on projects with other leading fashion schools, with French institutions (2008 'Metamorphoses' project at the Musée du Quai Branly) or with companies, amongst others, IFF, designing individual fragrances associated to the students' final collections.

Insitute of Fashion Design, Basel
The one, universally valid way to design professional, state-of-the-art fashion doesn't exist. We develop different positions and criteria with the students for a professional design practice in fashion. This includes exploring how the formative design process becomes visible through the collection and representation and what qualities are evoked by these means.

Rejecting a marketing-dominated development of uniform fashion products and representations we search for unique ways of design process praxis. Ways for the development of diversity and actual quality in products, services or technical procedures that are designed for people.

We consider fashion as worthwhile when it communicates positions independent of marketing industry dogmas and is meaningful in relation to a specific context. From this perspective it is possible to achieve relevant criteria in the design process and production, richness of artistic expression, as well as compelling representation, allowing a culture of design to unfold with the best understanding of the field.

IUAV University of Venice / Università IUAV di Venezia
The Undergraduate Degree Programme in Fashion Design of IUAV University of Venice aims at excellence. It intends not only to compete with the greatest fashion schools worldwide, training designers able to face the challenges of global fashion, but also to contribute to the formulation of a modern Italian Fashion, one capable of addressing the complexities and peculiarities of Italy within global fashion. The curriculum of this course directed by Maria Luisa Frisa is structured to train designers capable of conceptualizing, designing and creating fashion collections. Students are required to use different fashion tools and means of communication, as well as to develop a critical understanding of fashion as a cultural system. With an international staff of professors and industry specialists, this didactic curriculum mixes design and laboratory work with theoretical classes. The course encourages students to draw connections between individual and team-work and to design for handicraft as well as industrial production.

During the three years of the course, students acquire fundamental techniques and notions that allow them to manage complete projects designing garments and accessories and to present and communicate about their creations. Design and project labs are the heart of this training; while students are taught theoretically the procedures of Design in classrooms, this teaching becomes effective only when it can be applied to personal projects. This programme admits a total of 60 EU students, plus 5 non-EU.

The Graduate Degree Programme in Fashion Design and Theories, initiated in 2010 and coordinated by Mario Lupano, provides students with high-level skills and cultural knowledge. Through 'advanced workshops in fashion design', its didactic approach gives relevance to both theoretical and design issues. Experimentation carried out in these workshops aims to deal with complex and pressing contemporary issues highlighted by research produced in collaboration with the industry, private companies and public institutions. This programme admits a total of 20 students.

Jiangnan University, School of Textile and Clothing, Wuxi
The School of Textiles and Clothing of Jiangnan University was formed by the merging of the School of Textiles of Textile Engineering of Wuxi University of Light Industry and the Department of Textiles and Design of Jiangnan College. The history of the School can be traced back to 1952, when the Wuxi School of Textile Industries was established. Approved by the Ministry of Education, Jiangnan University belongs to the national '211 Project' and brings the development of the School of Textiles and Clothing into a new era.
The School offers a unique range of courses, covering Textile Engineering, Textile Chemical Engineering, Clothing Design and Engineering for the undergraduate program. Textile science and engineering is one of the key disciplines at Jiangnan University. The University has spent millions on an extensive range of advanced facilities to enhance teaching and research excellence within the School. The School was listed No.4 in the national ranking of textile science and engineering.

The School has been developing new strategies for providing professionally and administratively orientated courses to ensure that graduates are highly successful specialists with broadened knowledge and well-honed skills in textile engineering, textile chemistry and clothing engineering. At present, the total number of full time students has reached 1700, including 1500 undergraduates, and 200 postgraduates studying for master's degrees and doctoral degrees.

Lasalle College of the Arts, Singapore
Lasalle College of the Arts offers Southeast Asia's widest range of diploma and degree programmes focusing on areas including film, musical theatre, fine arts and fashion design. Since the college's inception in 1984, students from countries like India, China, Australia, France and Indonesia have benefited from the global industry experience of our educators and teaching methods that encourage interdisciplinary collaboration. Graduates draw on Asia's rich and diverse cultural

heritage for inspiration as they build ties with the region's network of artisans. They also participate in local creative projects as Singapore realises its goal of becoming a global arts city.

The BA (Hons) Fashion Design programme provides students with both a holistic understanding of the culture, context and professional practice of fashion, as well as a specialist perspective: students begin sharing common modules before choosing one of four pathways in Fashion Communication, Fashion Design, Fashion Management and Fashion Textiles, where they will develop, implement and realise creative concepts and marketable products. The Fashion Design pathway aims to develop in students an innovative and contemporary approach to fashion design. Workshops with international visiting practitioners, group critiques and tutorials equip students with the skills and knowledge to operate as creative designers and leaders in the fashion industry. Students will also experiment with inventive design methods and garment construction techniques to realize their fashion concepts. Industry-linked projects will further prepare fashion students for the newly expanding creative industry and market of Southeast Asian within a global context.

Musashino Art University, Tokyo

The fashion course at 'Musabi"s Department of Scenography, Display and Fashion is a course within a course: it addresses fashion as an artistic discipline within the context of 3-D environmental design. This course is uniquely structured to include a number of practices concerned with lifestyle theory and everyday life aesthetics; a concept expressed in Japanese as 'i-shoku-ju-yu', literally 'clothing, nutrition, living and entertainment'.

Kazuko Koike and Takashi Sugimoto, two founding directors of the lifestyle concept store MUJI, have been the driving force behind the course. Kazuko Koike, recognized as one of few contemporary Japanese fashion visionaries and a respected author on contemporary clothing, started the course in 1988 and remains today, following her retirement in 2005, a respected advisor. The department is currently headed by internationally renowned interior designer Takashi Sugimoto. His work relies on the use of primitive, brut and almost paganistic materials and volumes.

The two years of interdisciplinary teaching concerned with the environment includes: interior design, lighting, stage design, TV set production, furniture design and fashion. This allows, in the first year, cross-departmental projects with other fine art students, inland or abroad, in particular with Finland and France. In the third year, students must choose their vocational discipline.

Seminars are only loosely planned in our curriculum and their formats are not predetermined, allowing for a varied range of expression. Competition amongst students and professors makes for a healthy and exciting creative sparring. As an Art in Fashion course our focus is the thinking behind the work. Within an ever-changing and multifaceted fashion landscape, our intention is to teach and develop a fashion and a discourse that both complements and challenges the prevailing dogmas. Our students are therefore not required to produce a fashion collection in the classic sense, but rather to create a 3-D experience to which the clothing of the human body is central.

Omsk School of Fashion Design (OSFD), Omsk

The repeated success of graduates from a school must be explained by its teaching.

The OSFD, Omsk School of Fashion Design, established in 1977 is the oldest fashion design school in western Siberia. Many OSFD tutors today, are graduates from these early days. Their own creativity and passion and the remote geographic location of the school contribute to a unique learning environment and promote a culture of excellence. Today OSFD graduates are not only able to find positions with well-known Russian design companies and fashion houses but – thanks to the exposure of the school through the performance of its students in international design competitions – also internships in France, Italy and the UK.

The OSFD promotes self-sufficiency: a sophisticated approach to fashion education. Garment design is a complex process relying upon many elements: the laws of composition, colour, form interpretation and the rules of proportions. This design practice must be supported by in-depth knowledge of apparel technology, pattern drafting, fashion draping, modeling and surface treatments.

The OSFD relies on a combination of the theoretical design knowledge and philosophy and practical skills to support a stereotype-breaking approach to garment design. Knowledge and professionalism are at the core of our students' performance.

Our graduates are self-started individuals with passion and motivation. The sound fashion design knowledge that the OSFD brings them allows them to be at the cutting edge of the fashion industry.

Parsons The New School for Design, School of Fashion, New York

The School of Fashion is renowned for the strength of its curriculum, which develops graduates with exceptional conceptual, design, technical, and marketing skills who combine aesthetic refinement with commercial savvy. Students in all four programs develop distinctive aesthetic sensibilities along with diverse points of view that reflect the industry they will one day join. At Parsons, design exists within the context of the world and society, simultaneously embracing the past and challenging the future. Sustainable design stands at the core of the school's thinking. The school's four programs push students to question everything and to generate relevant and groundbreaking concepts.

Today, the School of Fashion stands at the crossroads of design thinking and innovative product development in the form of ideas, concepts, and clothing. The school provides students with the industry knowledge and vocabulary they need to succeed while fostering a desire to bring about positive change in society. As students learn to excel in design, they are encouraged to look outside the immediate context of fashion design and marketing to assess the needs of the ever-changing global economy and provide sustainable design solutions for the future.

The Royal Academy of Fine Arts, Artesis Hogeschool, Antwerp

The Antwerp Royal Academy of Fine Arts, founded in 1663, is one of the oldest of its kind in Europe. Owing to the post-war shifts in arts education, the 1960s saw the opening of several new applied arts departments including, in 1963, the fashion department under the leadership of Mary Prijot. The 1980s saw a transition in its teaching of fashion, away from the classic Parisian training and aesthetic towards an exploratory and conceptual approach encouraged today by our director Walter Van Beirendonck, himself a former student.

The Academy seeks to balance realism and creativity, avant-garde and tradition. Its intensive four-year degree gives students in-depth designing and making skills through projects and yearly collections complemented by theoretical classes, including fashion history and theory, art history, sociology and philosophy. Conceptual thinking is nurtured to help students move beyond 'just fashion' to the school's understanding of fashion creation as a process of experimentation, research, and adventure… a narrative way of working typical of the Academy.

While respecting our traditional practices and maintaining our individual character our teaching is evolving and adapting to the changing (fashion) world. Many ex-students teach at the academy, demonstrating our tight-knit ethos and contributing to a sense of continuity. Unlike many colleges we have worked hard to maintain a unique student/teacher relationship. 70 students are admitted in the first year and on average 12 graduates in year 4. While students go through rigorous training, tutors get to know them as people in their own right, to know their way of thinking and methodology. In turn this allows the tutors to guide them in a personal and individual way.

Thanks to the success of the course we have developed strong relationships with the industry including H&M, Dries Van Noten, Stephen Jones and Olivier Rizzo. We strive to prepare our student for a career in fashion without imposing anything 'specific' on their work, their collections remain personal journeys, engaged with but not determined by an industry project.

Ryerson University, the School of Fashion, Toronto

For over 60 years, the School of Fashion at Ryerson has been developing professionals in the fields of fashion design, communication and culture. As an international leader in fashion education, our academically and artistically demanding program focuses on fashion as an art, as a business and as an intellectual challenge. Today our alumni dominate the Canadian fashion industry and are rapidly gaining an international reputation.

Through global initiatives, exchange agreements and membership of the International Foundation of Fashion Technology Institutes (IFFTI), Ryerson is recognized as one of the top fashion undergraduate schools worldwide. In 2010, it introduced a MA degree in Fashion, the first of its kind in Canada.

The undergraduate program, leading to a Bachelor of Design, has two pathways: Fashion Design and Fashion Communication. In Fashion Design, students develop the vision and technical knowledge to design and produce garments for a variety of trends and needs. Its curriculum produces technically brilliant, business- and culture-savvy designers for both the couture and prêt-à-porter markets. The curriculum for Fashion Communication focuses on teaching students how to communicate trends and ideas with technical training in graphic design, illustration, photography, product development and marketing. Students on both pathways have the option to pursue Minors in the areas of business communication, entrepreneurship and innovation, marketing and retail and services management.

The Master of Arts in Fashion program focuses on interdisciplinary research/ studio experiences and offers a core mix of theoretical and practical courses. An internship program leads to an advance-level project or paper. The faculty's own scholarly research and creative activities helps to support students' work with a wide range of approaches including graphic and fashion design, health, ethics and sustainability, education, retail, publishing, museum and historical studies, ethnology, performing arts, computer gaming, digital technology, interactive media, photography and popular culture.

Working with the Theatre students in the university, the School of Fashion at Ryerson produces the largest fashion show in Canada, Mass Exodus, attended by nearly 5000 spectators each spring including industry leaders, retailers and media.

University of Wales, Newport

At University of Wales, Newport, we believe that today's cultural and economic diversity must impact our fashion design practice. In this age of excess, multiple-choices and individualism, fashion products must be built around innovation, aesthetic and design qualities. In an increasingly international environment, the pattern of collaborative practice predicted for fashion design highlights the diversity of professional and creative skills required.

Fashion designers must possess a wide portfolio of skills and demonstrate the ability to direct a project from its 2-D design at inception to a 3-D interpretation and to its final promotion in a way that is sensitive and pertinent to a specified market. Individual creativity, increased flexibility, resourcefulness and realism will be key qualities required of future designers as a rapidly changing workplace seeks a self-reliant, independent and self-motivated workforce. We encourage our students to creatively explore their individual talents through the demonstration of high analytical and technical skills but also to develop team working skills and an appreciation of the design process, of predicted future trends and of new technologies.

Although the curriculum of the fashion degree is focused on fashion design it also has a broad appreciation of any creative project and finds value in conceptual, abstract or experimental ideas, in critical conceptualizations, in the use of new technologies and in innovative collaborations. We believe that fashion is not just about clothing but about people and increasingly, through consumer customization and new creative partnerships made possible by technology, it ought to celebrate the individual.

What is your vision of fashion's future? In 2010, our brief for the final collections asked for 'vision tempered with reality'. This vision could be inspired by a number of things: body, mind, fabric, space, experience, emotion. Trained to think and to question, to challenge, discuss and defend your design ideas we hope to help our students to realise their 'vision'. Come and find your creative voice at Newport.

Winchester School of Art, Winchester

When asked why they have chosen to follow the Fashion and Textiles Design programme at Winchester School of Art, students mention: employment opportunities, the school's reputation, the quality of the equipment and the possibility to explore different subjects, either fashion, knitwear, printed or woven textiles before specializing. Our first year interdisciplinary approach helps students in the agonizing choice of which area of the fashion and textile industry to study. During this introductory year, a series of subject-specific projects allow exploration of different areas, while specialist workshops enable students to select and build their skills set. This approach encourages interdisciplinary synergies and learning practices more consistent with industry contexts.

Through the remainder of the programme students are encouraged to develop the broad range of practical knowledge and skills necessary for their chosen area of study. Knowledge of the evolving state-of-the-art equipments, techniques and methods employed by the creative industries is promoted by our curriculum. It supports in particular digital approaches to making and presentation alongside other industry standard technologies. Important traditional processes and a hands-on approach continue to be at the core of all training at Winchester School of Art, with skills such as pattern-cutting, draping and modelling, construction and use of industrial machines not being ignored.

We also understand that the design industry increasingly values employees that can demonstrate combinations of broad-based knowledge and specialist skills and that it seeks adaptable graduates, capable of multi-tasking creative projects and working in teams. To facilitate learning consistent with attaining such attributes, the Fashion and Textile Design programme includes interdisciplinary team experiences through shared live projects, student exchanges with other international universities, presentation skills appropriate to a range of industries and practical experience of contemporary technology used to attain design solutions.

ACKNOWLEDGEMENTS

I would like to thank everybody at Laurence King Publishing for making this book possible, in particular Helen Rochester for commissioning the project, Anne Townley for her guidance, Sophie Wise for her finishing touch and Kim Sinclair for the book's production. My thanks also go to the designer Melanie Mues.

I underestimated the task I undertook with this project. The moral support of my personal readers Charlotte Hetzel-Green, Stephanie Bull and Gayle Atkins has kept me going and their help in refining text and content has been greatly appreciated.

The student work in this book contributes to its impact. I would like to thank each of the extremely gifted student designers featured for entrusting me with their work – I hope to have done it justice. I wish every success for the future to: Alexandre Fléveau, Andrea Tramontan, Bernice Chua, Camille Bellot, Cathy Amouroux, Claire Tremlett, Cristina Sabaiduc, Dez Bara (Désiré Bara-Assi), Guillaume Dollinger, Irene Corazza, Janosch Mallwitz, Juliette Alleaume, Kai Ryosuke, Katya Babenko, Leony Aneston, Louise Tredwin, Lucy Zhang Shuai, Mariel Manuel, Marilou Dadat, Matthieu Thouvenot, Sean Cabezas, Sintija Reinfelde, Sophie Willett, Tatyana Kobikova, Tina Aileen, Tsolo Munkh (Tsolmandakh Munkhuu), Valentine Cloix, Verena Zeller and Verity Pemberton.

I would also like to thank all the tutors who have overseen this project. Their time, patience and contributions have been invaluable. Their passion and attentive care as fashion educators is very tangible and I hope it is reflected here. Thank you Bernadine Murray, Cyrille Chardon, David Meyer, Dominique Savard, Francoise Payot, Gabriele Monti, Gayle Atkins, Howard Tangye, Jean-Paul Longavesne, Lei Shen, Lionel Roudaut, Louise Pickles, Maria Luisa Frisa, Marina Timofeeva, Martin Blum, Michele Wesen-Bryant, Nellie Nooren, Patrick Ryan, Patrick Teypaz, Priska Morger, Robert Ott, Sharon Rees, Sharon Williams, Valeska Schmidt-Thomsen and Walter Van Beirendonck.